LITTLE GREEN APPLES
God Really Did Make Them!

LITTLE GREEN APPLES
God Really Did Make Them!

O.C. SMITH AND JAMES SHAW

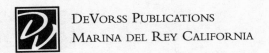
DeVorss Publications
Marina del Rey California

Little Green Apples

DeVorss & Company, *Publishers*
Box 550
Marina del Rey CA 90294-0550

www.devorss.com

Printed in the United States of America

TABLE OF CONTENTS

"O.C.'s music and the church were always one and the same. He and his music were like a bridge between God's love and life; they were inseparable. O.C. was the face of love and the sound of love, he brought an understanding of God's love to the world and sang it out for all to hear. O.C.'s presence is and will always be with me."

Nancy Wilson
Legendary Jazz Singer

"OC always brought comfort and wisdom. I'm forever indebted!"

Mike Garrett
1965 Heisman Trophy Winner

"Little Green Apples is O.C.'s love song, which he has left for us to learn exactly how to 'sing and dance' our way out of every kind of negative, limited condition, and "expand to God" and receive greater love, joy, success, and prosperity."

Rev. Ike
United Church Center in New York City

"My friendship with O.C. Smith spans over 50 years. Since the early 1950's when we worked together with Count Basie's band, O.C.'s warmth, beautiful voice, and sincere heart have been his spiritual trademark throughout his life and ministry."

Mike Stoller
co-writer of numerous hit songs for Elvis Presley, Peggy Lee, the Coasters, and the Drifters

"O.C. and I became good friends because we not only walked the rough side of the mountain together, but we also reached the top together. He was spiritual and loving, and I was blessed to call him my friend."

Della Reese
TV star, singer, author and minister

"O.C. had a global love and compassion for humankind. Whenever he came to the airport to get me not only did he tip generously but he also spent time talking and sharing with whoever crossed his path. He was never too busy to spend time with anyone. Just the thought of his infectious smirk and jolly laugh could bring a smile to anyone who knew him. O.C. my brother, my friend, my counselor, my pastor, your presence is with me forever and with all whom you love and who love you."

Dr. Barbara King
*minister, author, lecturer and Founder/Pastor
of Hillside Chapel and Truth Center, Atlanta*

"O.C. Smith was very special and I count myself as being very fortunate to have been special to him. If I had a problem, it didn't matter when I called. He simply reminded me that it was merely a hurdle that I had to overcome. I'll always love him, and miss his friendship."

James Janisse
Popular Southern California jazz radio broadcaster at KJJZ

"Reverend Dr. Smith's legacy will live on through the work he did, the friends he made and the lives he touched."

Gray Davis
Governor of California

"We remember with love his music. His heart and soul were felt by all who heard him, whether on stage or in church. They were filled with love. We remember with love his gentle nature. Confidently, yet lovingly, he lived the message he taught. We remember with love his dedication to things of the Spirit. His life touched many lives and inspired them to become what God created them to be."

Dr. Johnnie Colemon
minister, author, lecturer and Founder/Pastor of
Christ Universal Temple, Chicago

"The passing of Dr. O.C. Smith is a great loss to everyone involved. His life's work and contributions are part of a legacy he leaves for all to emulate."

James K. Hahn
Mayor of Los Angeles

"He gave up popular success in the music world, an outstanding musician and entertainer, to become an outstanding spiritual leader in the community – a warm, caring and firm pastor."

Los Angeles County Board of Supervisors

"... exemplary achievements and outstanding contributions ..."

Congress of the United States, US House of
Representatives,
Memorial Resolution Honoring Rev. Dr. O.C. Smith

FOREWORD

by Wally Amos
Inventor of "Famous Amos Chocolate Chip Cookies"

Truth is truth in any form and has been for centuries. It's not that we don't know what truth is; more often than not, we just do not know how to apply it in our own lives.

Little Green Apples: God Really Did Make Them! presents some truths in a simple, easy-to-digest format that will help you realize your dreams and achieve your goals. I found it to be a very practical book with a lot of "ah-ha!" moments. (Those are the moments when truth reveals itself to you in a very clear and common-sense way.) In many ways this book will jar your memory and help you remember some basic truths you have known all along.

Isn't it interesting that O. C. Smith's claim to fame was a song called *(God Didn't Make) Little Green Apples*? Years later, after many life experiences, ministerial school, and teaching, O. C. discovers that God made everything! As a result of all his life's lessons and teachings, that idea then becomes the foundation of a book called *Little Green Apples: God Really Did Make Them!*

Therein, I believe, lies the strength of this book. The information is built on sound spiritual laws, which are tried and true. They are laws that have been used in every possible situation with positive results. People of all races, sexes, colors, sizes—you name it—have used them and they have still produced positive results. They are laws that do not care how much money you have or how broke you might be. They *still* produce positive results. The bottom line is, they work if *you* work them.

So then: what will you do with this valuable information you are about to digest? Will this be just another book that you read and return to the shelf with all the other books you've read?

I suggest you treat this one differently.

Don't just read it. Let the ideas become a part of your deepest consciousness. Breathe them; incorporate them into every aspect of your daily life. Let these ideas become as habitual as walking and talking, so that you do not have to think about applying them—they just happen naturally.

When you can begin to do that, you will see a wonderful and powerful transformation in every area of your life. You won't just see God everywhere—there will be no place where you *cannot* see God! Then you can enjoy those apples!

This book can change your life. Get ready for that transformational experience!

Aloha,

Wally

Wally Amos is an author ("The Cookie Never Crumbles: Inspirational Recipes for Everyday Living"; "You Have the Power"; "Let Go, Let God"; "Watermelon Magic" and many others); speaker; and world-famous entrepreneur, now embarking on a new enterprise, Uncle Wally's Muffins.

PREFACE

Rev. O. C. Smith: A Letter to My Spiritual Father, Mentor and Friend

Dear O. C.:

Thank you so very much for being my spiritual father, mentor, and friend. Your teaching ministry provided me the principles for transforming my life completely. You taught me how to alter my outlook, change my mind, and keep the change. Genuine compassion replaced my affinity for criticism. I kicked my addictions to the dry, sterile emotional deserts of anger, resentment, and cynicism and stepped out into the oases of happiness, excitement, optimism, and trust. As faith replaced my fears, unlimited joy supplanted my years-old depression.

You taught me that in the silence of my mind is God; I learned to feel the Creator's pulse in the beat of my heart. Breaking through the ice banks of my ignorance, I soon noticed that people and events around me seemed to change—for the better. My friends and business associates increased and the holes in my social calendar filled up with people to see, places to go, and things to do—both a natural result of my changing spirituality and its evidence.

As a public school law consultant and a social researcher with a zealous voice and a jaundiced eye, I learned from you—when we both participated in Littleton, Colorado, as invited speakers for a memorial to slain Columbine High School students—that compassion, not passion alone, will provide the greatest good for the greatest number. Though I love the law, I now know it is the law of love that will save us all. Through your teachings, you showed me the bonds that enslaved me to religious dogma and gave me the keys to my own freedom; you reminded me that it is with my own consent that I am either my own slave or my own savior.

Through your wonderful classes at M. E. C. C. A. (Metaphysical Evolvement Center at City of Angels), at our wonderful City of Angels Church of Religious Science, I learned that God dwells in me instantly and constantly and, more important, *chooses* to do so. Your weekly teachings and expert structuring of the M. E. C. C. A. curriculum led me to the truth, the whole truth, and nothing but the truth. With love and great patience you taught me and everybody else at City of Angels Church that by saving our own spiritual lives—as God intended and the Master Teacher Jesus instructed and demonstrated—we, and the rest of humanity, could save the entire world.

Convincing me of my own *Divinity-Identity*, rather than converting me to any doctrine, was the backbone of your teaching. You taught me not to fear the voice of God within me, but to learn to recognize it and love the syntax and sense of Divine Spirit. From you I learned that God is both the source of my supply and the supply itself. I marveled at your counsel that the answer to any problem *must* be of a higher order and greater than the problem itself. *Live in the answer—don't loiter in the problem. Soar to the solution, don't sink to the problem.* More than mere lip-service, these words were stout planks in your strong platform, sharpened arrows in your spiritual quiver. And, expert archer that you were, your aim always found its target, in your ministry and your own mastery of life.

Your absolute fearlessness without the fakery of arrogance showed that truly understanding and negotiating life is an art better achieved by omitting the artificial. Your boldness in proclaiming the truth about humankind's spirituality was matched by the absence of braggadocio about your personal, legendary achievements. You sang and sermonized about love, joy, peace, and goodness and gave me the melodies to make my own music. You showed me the way even as you showed me how to get out of my own way.

Your praise was genuine and generous, your humility as real as your honesty. When you told me of your idea for this book, saying you needed me to be your co-writer, I was especially pleased and honored. On this particular 'track' of life, we were teammates running the relay. *SUDDENLY, YOU HANDED ME THE BATON!*

O. C., your rich baritone voice and hit songs touched an inspired a generation. Our book, too, will help reveal to present and future generations their true spiritual song in the key of life. A good and faithful servant, you performed your life's work on earth fully and so very well. I know that God has richly and abundantly blessed you with your next assignment and that, in fulfilling it, you are singing your biggest song yet.

With eternal gratitude and love,

Your friend, student, and writing partner,

Jim Shaw

ACKNOWLEDGMENTS

I want to acknowledge, first and foremost, my creator, best friend, and all-knowing guide: God. Through my friend Betty Eadie, who is publisher of another work of mine, I have learned to find God, instantly and everywhere, by being willing to *think* a conversation (yes) in mind. Betty Eadie emphasizes in her marvelous book *Embraced by the Light* that we do not have to wait until a particular day of worship to talk to God. We can talk to God, and God is willing to listen to anything we have to say, at any time at all. And a conversation once a week is simply not enough.

My car radio used to be my constant traveling companion. Ever since I read and understood what Eadie meant, though, I have been keeping the radio *off* more than on. During these times, in the silence of my mind, I talk to God. At all times, God answers. As a result, I know more about myself and my purpose in life than I ever have before. The willingness to engage in conversations with God, about everything, heavy and light, formal and informal, serious and funny, has given me an understanding of life that I never had before. The static in that radio between my ears has diminished considerably as my conversations with God have increased. That noise has given way to God's welcome news about me—and all creation.

The earth angel of my life is my wife, Sylvia, my friend, my partner, and my soul mate. Her understanding of the rigors of the writer's life and my chronic bouts of being surrounded by unseen yet ubiquitous clouds of words, ideas, and concepts is as much appreciated as it is miraculous. At the time of this writing, we have been married for 24 years. She has blessed and changed my life, and enabled me to see and believe what she has always seen in me.

Sylvia's and my children, Jimmy, Lawrence, and Aaron, are bundles of joy, boundless energy, and consummate curiosity whose open outlooks on life and whose grade school level candor and expressiveness constantly teach and remind me who the real treasures in life really are. The scriptural "A little child shall lead them" is an apropos description of Jimmy, Lawrence, and Aaron's cherubic effects on our household, my life, and my work.

To David, my brother, who always took time to listen to my ideas and show interest in my work, despite his own feats of strength, documented in *The Guinness Book of World Records,* and outstanding contributions in the corporate sector, as well as working to help others achieve higher levels of physical and psychological well-being: Thank you for caring.

I am indebted to Arthur Vergara, publisher at DeVorss & Company, for his comprehensive grasp of subject matter and the requisites that make a writer "complete"; and for his ability to anticipate the turns in the road before I have even seen the road itself. Were it not for his eagle eye and laser-sharp mind, substance and style might never have met in this volume. Arthur, I deeply appreciate your prodigious gifts and how you use them. You can make any writer a better writer.

Gary Peattie, chief operating officer at DeVorss & Company, believed in this project from the beginning. I am grateful that he, too, saw it desirable and necessary to make available to the reading public the wonderful truths that comprised Rev. O. C. Smith's dynamic and life-transforming ministry.

Debbie Krovitz, Direct Marketing Manager at DeVorss & Company, possesses marketing instincts and a well-honed understanding of the various climes of the literary marketplace that give her an expertise to make any publisher proud. I am grateful to her for all she does to place this work in the hands of as many readers as possible.

Rev. Helen Jones, minister and practitioner of the City of Angels Church of Religious Science, taught me in her class that good is both the reason for and result of everything; and that good is present even when our awareness of it is not. Thank you, Reverend Helen.

Dr. Maisha Hazzard, in her class at the City of Angels Church of Religious Science, taught me that once a person places faith in God, there is no force that can counter the absolute and Divine power that results. Thank you, Dr. Maisha, for helping me to address the Creator in full, unreserved faith; to move in mind and in Spirit; and, most important, to get my bloated human-ness and its "reasonable doubts" out of the way.

Mrs. Robbie Smith is a brave and courageous woman who continues on with the vital work of the City of Angels Church of Religious Science, the church she co-founded with Rev. Dr. O. C. Smith. Without her desire to see this book published and her support for my finishing the writing of it, and my taking the "baton" across the finish line, this book would not have been. It is so because she would have it so. *Robbie, thank you so very much!*

James Shaw

"LITTLE GREEN APPLES"

In 1968 a popular song streaked across the musical firmament like a comet blazing through the heavens. Within hours of its being broadcast over the nation's radio stations, delighted listeners could be heard humming, singing, and whistling it. Calling up radio stations and requesting the song became a favorite pastime.

That song, "Little Green Apples," earned a Grammy award, pop music's highest honor, and gave its artist, O. C. Smith, a number-two place on both the pop and R&B charts. The recording went on to become a worldwide sensation, selling multiple millions of copies and winning a Grammy nomination for O. C.

The song's title is a figure of speech reflecting the singer's wish to persuade a listener of the truth of what he sings. The singer croons his gratitude for all the attention and affection he receives from the angelic and devoted wife and mother he praises. Fearing he'll be doubted, he sings, "And if that's not loving me / Then all I've got to say [is] / God didn't make / Little green apples"—something he knows his listener won't disbelieve.

The book you are holding owes its title to that song, so identified with O. C. Smith that it is referred to as his "signature song." The renowned singer was also the co-writer of this book in his capacity as the Reverend Doctor O. C. Smith, a role to which he felt called over and beyond his musical career. "Once the connection was made," he later observed, "it was all-consuming."

The book's title, with its reference to the block-buster song, suggests an unshakable belief in an all-loving God, more wonderful than we humans have words to describe, whose presence, power, and purpose, are instantly and constantly available to us, and working for us. The book reveals what God's "little green apples" are and, further, that they are both our divine inheritance and the keys to our destiny. God's little green apples are exclusively ours for the picking. As true as the tree in the orchard of life in which they abound, these "green apples" can change and shape your life, helping you to surmount every obstacle and realize your every dream.

Read on…they are waiting for you to harvest them.

LITTLE GREEN APPLES

words and music by Bobby Russell

And I wake up in the morning
With my hair down in my eyes and she says "Hi"
And I stumble to the breakfast table
While the kids are going off to school…goodbye
And she reaches out and takes my hand
And squeezes it and says "How ya feelin', hon?"
And I look across at smiling lips
That warm my heart and see my morning sun

And if that's not loving me
Then all I've got to say

God didn't make
Little green apples
And it don't rain
In Indianapolis
In the summertime
And there's no such thing
As Doctor Seuss
Or Disneyland
And Mother Goose
No nursery rhyme

God didn't make
Little green apples
And it don't rain
In Indianapolis
In the summertime
And when my self
Is feeling low
I think about
Her face aglow
And ease my mind

LITTLE GREEN APPLES

Sometimes I call her up at home knowing she's busy
And ask her if she could get away and meet me
And maybe we could grab a bite to eat
And she drops what she's doing
And she hurries down to meet me
And I'm always late
But she sits waiting patiently and smiles
When she first sees me
'Cause she's made that way

And if that ain't loving me
Then all I've got to say

God didn't make
Little green apples
And it don't snow
In Minneapolis
When the winter comes
And there's no such thing
As make-believe
Puppy dogs
Autumn leaves
And BB guns

God didn't make
Little green apples
And it don't rain
In Indianapolis

LITTLE GREEN APPLES
God Really Did Make Them!

CHAPTER 1

YOUR GOLD MIND

LIFE IS MORE BEAUTIFUL than we have ever imagined or could ever imagine it to be. When we open our eyes and look around us, there is an abundance of every good thing. There are endless and countless varieties of plants and animals, and every form and variation of life.

The Great Teacher Jesus said, "It is the Father's good pleasure" to give us every good thing. What a wonderful statement that is! It is both a promise and a declaration. Great spiritual leaders of various religions, in some form or other, have voiced the same truth. God's desire is to give us what we desire. God has created Life as a banquet. The table has been set with a multitude of good; that good always multiplies.

God is the Host and we are the guests. Put another way, every day that we awaken is like hitting the jackpot in the Lotto Grand Lottery. God's goods have already been given to us: our Lotto ticket *already* contains the winning numbers. It is up to us to surrender that ticket and cash it in. That requires desire, intention, motivation, and effort on our part. Although life is indeed a banquet, God has arranged His wondrous and abundant feast for us as a *buffet* on a grand and sumptuous table.

The writer Stretton Smith explains that this means the food won't, on its own, come to us. We must *walk* over to it, *pick* up a plate and *serve* ourselves. In other words, we must think the thoughts, take the steps, and reach out and *grasp* the good that awaits us. And we must do this time and again, for the entirety of our lives. If we don't do that, our good simply waits…and waits…and waits. Meanwhile, the pattern of our lives continues as it is. Despite the need or desire for change, it simply will not happen unless and until we take the right *action*.

Many people, through misinformation, miseducation, or misadventure, are conditioned to believe that life must be difficult in order to have meaning or value. There are some people who actually become uncomfortable when good comes their way, or when (as they say) "things are just too good." To them—and to paraphrase a popular slogan—without pain, there is no gain.

Some people, unable to stand peace and happiness, simply cannot resist "stirring up the waters" in their desire to create some "meaningful" tension and stress in their lives. Other people harbor suspicion and distrust when they get what they want sooner than they expect, or even when people treat them more kindly or generously than they feel they deserve to be treated. Still others, instead of being gloriously free, live entangled in assorted webs and snares.

These kinds of people are trapped in the attics of their own minds and look out upon the world through the cobwebs and other haze covering their vision. Convinced that life is limited, they limit their life. Instead of having genuine friendships and loving relationships, they prefer to rummage around in their life's cubicles, absorbing the must and dust and rust of ages and experiences past. Only after doing so do they allow themselves to face the world. Subsequently, they have a very limited, blurred, and cynical outlook on just about everything.

Your outlook reflects, reproduces, and is completely controlled by your "in-look": inner vision.

LIFE IS FOR YOU, BUT ARE YOU FOR LIFE?

By "greeting" life in this manner, they unknowingly block, delay, reduce, or cancel any good that might come their way. They persist in thinking that life is cold, tough, and conspiring against them; or that the stars are crossed in the heavens and the planets are not aligned; or that somebody else always gets life's goods because they have the "right stuff"—whatever that is. Sadly, they do not even *know*—and would never suspect—that *they* are their own roadblocks on life's "Success Highway 1."

One might say they are the victims of their own stinking thinking. For example, when a hand is extended to them, they withdraw and retreat, at least inside themselves; when somebody greets them with a smile, they beam insincerely or may even frown; when there is good news, they scarcely believe it. Skeptical about almost everything, they find it difficult to see themselves as beneficiaries and recipients of all the good that life has to offer. They constantly wonder or worry about the motives of others, and they let suspicion hover over their relationships, whether social or personal.

As a comedian once joked, these kinds of people even claim that the handwriting on the wall is a forgery! Trapped in the midst of their misery, they constantly miss out on the true joys and pleasures of living. Unwilling to step out and thrive in the sun, they seem

3

content merely to survive beneath the cover of their own shadows. The motion of their lives can be described as "circular"—that is, going around in circles.

Here is a biological fact that will illustrate the admittedly stark picture of these kinds of people's lives: a goldfish can be left in a fishbowl for a period of, say, six months. Afterwards it can be taken out of its bowl and put into the ocean. Despite its watery origins, though, it refuses to venture out and instead only circulates in an area of the exact circumference as its original fishbowl. *Yet it has the entire ocean for itself!*

Many people are scarcely much different from that. Although there is an infinite universe from which to draw, more often than not they fail to open themselves up to it and accept the abundant good that is theirs by "Executive Order." How can they—or anybody—be the earthly beneficiaries of "Heaven's Goods"? They first must have the mental equivalent of that which they desire to experience (be, do, and have). Cultivating this is a critically important prerequisite.

> *Just as you bathe your body, you can bathe your mind in rich, positive, powerful thoughts that will give your life a shine and luster beyond what ordinary soaps can do.*

What You See Is What You Get

Having the Mental Equivalent means having the ability to visualize or feel that what you want to experience is already a reality in your life: you accept the Mental Equivalent as truth. It is the mental representation of—

and embodies—the goal that you simultaneously embrace. It is constantly on your horizon, for you put it there. It is what beams light and excitement in your eyes as you picture in your mind the desired goal or experience fostered and focused by the Mental Equivalent.

Like the masterwork of a professional interior designer, the Mental Equivalent is the picture of your life exactly as you *design* it to be. As the late, great comedian Flip Wilson used to say, "What you see is what you get." Suppose a small child has three baskets or containers of jewelry placed in front of her, one being large baubles of costume jewelry; the other, real diamonds filling up two baskets. Generally, she will choose the large, worthless baubles. She seems unable to embrace mentally the idea that true riches are hers for the taking—in the next basket.

Adults think and act in much the same way, often choosing mostly the superficial, easy-to-grab yet worthless trinkets along life's paths. The true treasures, though obvious to some, seem hidden or too distant to so many others. Most people relate to life by thinking more about what they do not have than what they do have. As a consequence, they spend their lives thinking in terms of "wanting" and "needing." They are obsessed more about having those things that do *not* make life complete than about those that *do*. Life, to them, is a puzzle with holes instead of a *whole* puzzle. No matter how few those holes are, they nevertheless blind their eyes to the large, lush, and radiant canvas of the "bigger picture."

Accept the good that God has already provided you,
and SEE your life change before your very eyes.

THOUGHTS ARE THINGS

We cannot stop thinking. The mind is not like a light-switch that can be turned on and off. Every thought we think is a "suggestion" we make to ourselves. Researchers report that the average individual thinks about 40,000 thoughts per day, 85 percent of which are negative: worry, doubt, fear, resentment, anger, hate, frustration, jealousy, envy. We must consciously guard against allowing the mind to dwell on distasteful and harmful thoughts by keeping it under "surveillance," consciously being aware of the train of thoughts in which we allow it to engage. Thoughts become things, and those things become the realities of our life.

Our life is much like an automobile with its headlights on at night. Everywhere the light beams go, the car follows. Our life follows the direction in which our thoughts flow, whether they be positive or negative. The quality of life that flows through us is seen by us as either good or bad. Regardless of how we evaluate it, our life is the reality or sum total of the *kinds* of thoughts that, like a train, speed through the "depot" of our mind. The picture of our lives constantly rolls out and emerges before us, whether we see it at each "whistle stop" or not until the "final stop."

In the "theater of your mind, on the stage of your imagination" [from Rev. Ike], prop yourself up for life by changing the wardrobe of your mind. Life's doors will open and life itself will greet you with constant applause.

LIFE: SHAPE IT ANY WAY YOU LIKE

Life is much like the clay a potter uses for molding and shaping objects. She takes the clay and molds it into a plate, a vase, a human figurine, or an endless array of other objects. Similarly, we are constantly fashioning or molding our life's experiences by the decisions we make. Life is "for" us or "against" us based on what we *decide* (mold and shape) it to be. There is no outside force working against us or any system blocking us. We are the sculptor, and the thoughts we *hold* are the clay that becomes the mold for the shape and form of our lives. To change the shape of our lives, we must "break the mold" created by the habitual thoughts that occupy our mind.

If you want a bigger and better life, you must expand your thinking beyond the confines of the smaller mold, which contains or confines you, and practice a bigger and better quality of thinking. The great Albert Einstein once said that the thoughts leading to the answer to any of life's problems must be better than and superior to the original thoughts that created the problem in the first place.

There are "high grade" thoughts and "low grade" thoughts. High grade thoughts are positive and contain an energy that motivates you to take positive, progressive, and effective courses of action. Only positive thoughts will produce for you the higher quality of life—filled with unlimited and continuous abundance and good— that you desire. Since your thoughts contain energy, they can make your life *sink* or *soar*.

You have more power than any other species on the planet. Decide to use it creatively and positively.

You Are the Producer of Your Life Script

It has been said that by the time a child reaches the age of 5, he/she has heard the word "no" over 50,000 times. In this brief time span, then, the child has faced a virtual wall of "no's." That is the word every child is most familiar with yet the one he/she most detests. Children's behavior therefore becomes based on a constant expectation that any and all of their desires will meet resistance in the form of rejection, challenge, struggle—in other words, a stream of "no," "no," "no."

As children move toward adulthood, they hear a symphony of "no's" that orchestrates their whole approach to life and shapes and reinforces their negative point of view. Their personalities and outlook on life are the direct results of this conditioning, by-products of their mental and emotional reactions to their experiences. These become the foundation for the "life script" they are constantly acting out.

And so it is with all of us. Your mind is a motion picture production company. You "employ" script-writers, directors, producers, actors, and agents—and they are all YOU! Since you can't "fire" anybody, ALL your pictures get made. If you don't like the picture, you *are* the writer and you can change the script. You have the power to "rewrite" the thoughts that produce your life's picture.

Your value at life's "box office" goes up when you dare to change and rewrite your own life script.

YOUR TRUE NATURE

Two questions can be posed to people all over the planet, regardless of their race, class, culture, social, or economic background. These two questions could have been asked millions of years ago. They will be asked millions of years in the future. They can be asked throughout the cosmos. They can be asked today, and they can be asked right now. If they are answered honestly by whoever responds to them, the answer to these two questions will always be "Yes."

The first question is: "Don't you desire to have someone to love?" The second question is: "Don't you desire to have someone love you?" The answer to both questions is "Yes." Why? Because Love is the very essence and nature of the Intelligence that permeates the Universe. This Universal Intelligence has placed Itself in the innermost recesses of each of its creations.

Ignorant to a large degree about ourselves, we human beings en masse have instead known and engaged in wars and other forms of violence but have seldom labored with equal diligence to know the true nature of their being. Love is the true nature and essence of all life. As a species existing on this earth for millennia, we humans are only now beginning to understand that. We have sought high and low and hither and yon to discover our true nature, only to either express or experience pain, suffering, and despair. And the more we struggled to find our true nature, the more elusive it seemed to be.

There is an old Hindu story about a mythical god whose name was Brahma. One day he asked some of his scholars to sit with him and help him to determine a place where he might hide people's true nature—love—from them, in order that they would not abuse it any longer. One scholar suggested that he hide this love upon the highest mountain. Brahma thought for a moment and decided to veto the idea, because humankind has spaceships that go to the outer reaches of the universe, and one day, while cruising past the highest of earth's mountains, they would surely find their true self.

Another esteemed scholar suggested that Brahma hide people's love, their true nature, at the bottom of the deepest ocean. Brahma thought again and rejected that idea, too. He reasoned that humankind has nuclear submarines, and one day they would traverse the ocean floor and make the discovery.

Finally, a third scholar said, "I've got it, Brahma! Why don't you hide this love at the center of the earth?" Brahma thought for a moment and again said no, because he knew that people were always digging for gold, silver, diamonds, oil, and coal. He reasoned that one day, people would nearly exhaust the earth's supply of these precious minerals by digging only deeper. Then they would find their true nature. So hiding it in the core of the earth simply would not do.

Brahma knew, with all the understanding of the ages, that he had to find a place to hide this true nature where people would never think to look for it. Suddenly, a light went on in Brahma's mind, and he smiled. He told his scholars, "I've got it! I'll hide their true nature in a place where they will never think to look for love. I'll hide it *within* them!"

Our sole responsibility, as we journey through life, should be to turn away from the world of events, effects, situations, and circumstances and instead turn our attention within, in order that we may "drink" from the eternal fountain of love that never runs dry, thereby *re-creating* for ourselves the life that was intended and ordained for us in the beginning. A prominent reason we struggle is that we are often capsized in our emotional seas of hate, anger, doubt, resentment, and frustration. Underneath all of this is a deep and continuous sense of separation from God—the source of all good.

This sense of alienation and separation between us and God is the root cause of all of our problems. Not realizing that we were placed here to succeed, we instead suffer. Rejecting our birthright as victor over all our circumstances, we instead don the garb and enact the role of universal victim. Turning away from the power that God makes available to us, we turn instead into powerless, desperate beings, thinking life to be one massive, continuous headache. Our days spent in stress and struggle, our nights in fitful sleeplessness, we proclaim, with the "wisdom" of the perpetual failure, that "life is hard, then you die."

> *Discover am become your true nature. Share your love and shape your world.*

God's Instant and Eternal Gift to Us

At birth, each of us was given a priceless gift—our consciousness—to use in any manner that we choose. Unfortunately, the tides of humanity that have marched through the corridors of time gradually began to lose sight and awareness of this greatest of gifts, which is imbued with love. Instead, we as humans cultivated a dark outlook and began to see the world and view life as an endless struggle with a ceaseless array of difficulties and absurdities.

In our thinking we soon began to dwell primarily on the *weight* rather than on the *wealth* of life. Like Shakespeare's Hamlet, we feel we are driven from pillar to post, "betwixt and between," walking backwards into the future. Feeling cursed by the schizophrenia of "To be or not to be?" we bellow and blame and cry in shame. Our millennia-long failure to discover that life is *for* us exposes only *our* faults (not life's), our blind choices, and our gross misdeeds.

Since our life *is* in God's embrace, and since God gave us free and unfettered will (choice) in all our affairs, we *can* choose either to be *cursed* by the "weight" of life's heavy loads or *cured* by the magnificent majesty of God's great gifts created just for—and expressed *through*—us: love, joy, prosperity, happiness, peace, health, wholeness, abundance. God does not neglect us; it is we who neglect ourselves!

As I look back upon my career as an entertainer, I believe that during the Vietnam War, at a time when pain and suffering and anger and hatred were rife, many other entertainers, in addition to myself, sought to bring to the mass consciousness deep spiritual truths about ourselves, our purpose, and our destiny, singing songs with messages that dealt with love, peace, and the preservation of the earth.

Joan Baez; Crosby, Stills and Nash; Marvin Gaye; Peter, Paul, and Mary; and Harry Belafonte were some of the legions of entertainers who I believe were courageous channels through whom the Universal Intelligence expressed Itself, thus "alerting" human beings everywhere to our true nature: children of the Universal Intelligence, created from, and for, Love.

Through music, the universal language, countless hearts were healed, hope soared as if with wings, spirits were united, messages sent, and meanings received. Songs about love were balms for souls alienated by bombs and the politics of hate. "Make Love, Not War" was both mandate and mantra, spoken and shouted and sung by countless millions.

Until that period of the so-called "radical Sixties," never before in the history of humankind had love been so massively and publicly proclaimed as the solution to humanity's ills. America had turned on itself—like a dog on its tail—and many an entertainer's spiritual mission was to *return* anybody within hearing to his or her *true* loving, spiritual, peace-making self.

Return to your true Source, God, and watch your life take off with wings like an eagle.

VISION, NOT DI-VISION

The scripture says, "Physician heal thyself." The healing comes as the result of our seeing life not as we perceive (make that *deceive*) it to be, but as it truly is—totally and universally for us. The healing follows when we cease making an attempt to repair something that has never been broken: life itself. Regardless of what we do during the course of a day, whether we are employer or employee, nothing that we do during a given day is more important than beginning that day in a few moments of silence, visualizing our lives and the lives of every individual on this earth-plane filled with and expressing love. The ability to envision life the way we want it is a special gift from God.

As God took a world that the scriptures describe as "without form and void" and created it exactly the way God desired, we can also create our world according to the vision of it we have in our minds. All we need to do is *see* things the way God *intended* them to be. What then follows this envisioning is a flow of energy whose sole purpose is to bring about, or make real, our vision.

This energy—described by some as "cosmic," "universal," or "God energy"—is vital and contains tremendous force. Architects, graphic artists, athletes, and many others have long used it to place a desired vision in their *mindscape* so that the foundation (for the reality itself) is laid and brings forth and supports the *landscape*—the vision materialized. Going into prayer or meditation, and engaging in such envisioning, *unifies* you with God. Separation or *division* from God is the cause of the desperate, stunted, withered and cursed life.

Return to your true Source—God—and see life through the Creator's eyes.

THE GREATER AND THE LESSER

In my counseling sessions with individuals who are planning to get married, I share lessons on how important it is to maintain a consciousness of love. I make a statement to them that usually earns me a blank stare until I explain its meaning: "THE GREATER ALWAYS CONSUMES THE LESSER." I share with them that there is an invisible line called the Continental Divide that runs north and south throughout the U.S. All lakes, rivers, and streams east of the Divide flow into or toward the Atlantic Ocean; all those west of the Divide flow into or toward the Pacific. Remember: "The greater always consumes the lesser."

I share with them that there will be times in their marital experience together when they will have disagreements and that those disagreements must be thought of as lakes, rivers, and streams—*the lesser*—flowing into their love for each other which, like the ocean, is *the greater*. "The greater always consumes the lesser." This principle is applicable to any experience in our lives.

Love might be compared to water flowing down a mountainside and running into a barrier. When that happens, the water will flow around either side of the barrier until it creates a route (rivulet) to continue its journey down the mountain. Its journey cannot and will not be impeded. In reality, Love is the only power that girds up the entire Universe. It is more powerful than the most awesome and torrential waterfall; it is even older than the most ancient of streams. It is our natural state of being.

That's why we are *impelled* to say "Yes" to the two questions posed earlier. Every other form of expression that we experience in life is learned. For example, hate, anger, resentment are taught. They come from without (outside ourselves) and not from within. Only love comes from within. That is God's intent. That is the only way to change the harmful effects of the "outer emotions."

Love is the law. So be its best enforcer and uphold it.

SINGING IN THE KEY OF LOVE

I am often asked to sing or simply quote the wonderful lyrics of that hugely successful song I recorded, whose title this book reflects. "Little Green Apples," to me, is a pure love song. The lyrics are wholesome, inspirational, and self-explanatory. The melody is immensely comforting and uplifting. Let's take a brief look at some of those famous lyrics:

And I wake up in the mornin'
With my hair down in my eyes and she
says "Hi"
And I stumble to the breakfast table
While the kids are goin' off to school...
goodbye
And she reaches out 'n' takes my hand
And squeezes it 'n' says "How ya feelin',
hon?"
And I look across at smilin' lips
That warm my heart and see my mornin'
sun

And if that's not lovin' me
Then all I've got to say

God didn't make little green apples
And it don't rain in Indianapolis in the
summertime
And there's no such thing as Doctor Seuss
Or Disneyland, and Mother Goose, no
nursery rhyme
God didn't make little green apples
And it don't rain in Indianapolis in the

summertime
And when myself is feelin' low
I think about her face aglow and
ease my mind

—words and music by Bobby Russell

God, in an act of fathomless and indescribable love, created us from Its own self. It is that very *essence* and *presence* of God within us that moves some to write and sing songs of love.

It is the God Light radiating in us that is seen whenever we express and experience love. And we can consciously connect with that wonderful all-knowing and all-powerful Presence by going within, through prayer and meditation. Indeed, in order to advance in life, we *must* go within and avail ourselves of Divine inspiration and guidance. If we do not go within, then we go...without!

When you see someone without a smile, give them yours. Look at them through the God-light of your eyes.

Conscious Union with God

With every thought we think we are suggesting something to ourselves. The statement that we habitually place after the words "I am" eventually becomes our experience. For example, if we dwell on the idea that "I am sick," "I am poor," or "I am less than," etc., that is what we become. Instead, we must wisely confirm our Divinity-Identity by affirming, with confidence and high self-esteem, that "I am magnificent," "I am perfect," "I am whole," or "I am Divine."

There was a man who wanted to learn how to shoot a rifle. He went to a firing range one day and hired an expert to teach him. His instructor, after showing him the very basics of gun craft, then instructed him to observe carefully. The instructor repeatedly emptied the chamber of his gun into the automatic targets as they appeared one by one. Finally, he paused and said, "What do you think? Are you ready?" The would-be marksman said, "Yes, I think so."

He confidently unholstered his gun, and when the target came into view, he fired and didn't stop until his gun was empty. He looked at the target and blinked and shook his head. Stunned, he could not believe his eyes. Not only had he *not* hit the bull's eye, none of his bullets had hit the target anywhere at all. Confused, he turned to his instructor and asked, "Tell me, what could I be doing wrong?" The instructor replied, "You're aiming too low."

Too often, we aim low in life and then wonder why we seem to be scraping the bottom of the barrel and why life's paths seem full of treacherous twists and turns. Again, that is a consequence of our separating ourselves from God. We must elevate our minds and raise our vision to where God-on-High is. There is a reason why our Creator is often referred to as "God-on-High." There is no such thing as God-on-low! Why, then, do we persist in going *there*?

Let your spirit soar and you will find God. Keep company "on High" and watch so-called problems drop out of sight, unable to keep up with you.

LIVING AS YOU THINK, THINKING AS YOU LIVE

Of all the life forms inhabiting this earth plane, there is none other that has the conscious and deliberate ability to choose than ours. Our power of choice and decision to choose is the "feature" that distinguishes us from all other animals. The scriptures say that we humans have been given dominion over the fowl of the air, the fish in the sea, and the animals that crawl and walk on the earth.

If this is true—and it is—then it is necessary that we choose to take dominion over ourselves, our lives, and our emotions, and make certain that they are of the highest quality. For example, when we go to a store to shop for produce, we don't just randomly choose vegetables and fruits. We take time to choose the apples, oranges, tomatoes, eggplant, squash, and so forth. And we squeeze, thump, and pinch until we are satisfied that they not only *look* appealing and appetizing, but also *feel* robust and fresh enough to meet our standards.

Likewise, thought in all its forms is a function and expression of inspection and choice. We have the power to choose the thoughts, feelings, and emotions that serve us. Choice, then, is a powerful tool that we are always using, whether we realize it or not. We are always making choices, even when we think we are not. In other words, *not* making a choice is still a choice: *not* to choose.

In order for our lives to be upgraded and improved, we have to be consciously aware of, and pay attention to, the choices we make. Doing so automatically gives us the kind of *conscious control* that perhaps was lacking before. We have to inspect our thoughts and keep them under surveillance to make sure they are of the highest quality.

Like food, thoughts can spoil, rot, and become unhealthy, eventually making us sick.

Just as we have high standards for choosing the food we allow to occupy the vessel that is our stomach, we also must deliberately set and maintain high standards in choosing the kinds of thoughts we allow to occupy the vessel of our mind. New York's Empire State Building is one of the architectural marvels of this nation, attracting thousands of visitors each year. Many are fascinated by scaling the tall skyscraper and arriving on the Observation Deck high above the city. For them, it is a spectacular way to put the "Big Apple" in splendid perspective. In panoramic splendor they can see in an unlimited radius of 360 degrees, taking in the Hudson River; the states of New Jersey, Connecticut, and Pennsylvania; Staten Island; the Bronx; Manhattan; and more.

Needless to say, the experience is exhilarating. It is a highly visual and emotional one that is not disrupted by the clanging, jangling, jarring of the city some 1200 feet below. In marked contrast to this virtual "reaching-to-heaven" experience, however, is the inevitable descent into the depths of the smog, smell, grind, and smut that characterize the same city.

Just as we can choose to scale the Empire State Building, we can also choose to ascend to our highest levels of thought and view life from the "high tower" to which those thoughts take us. That is, we can choose to see an experience from the gutter or street level of our mind, where we find goop, garbage, graffiti, chaos, and confusion. Or we can choose to ascend and rise to the highest levels of consciousness—the observation deck—and view that same experience from an elevation where we find peace, harmony, joy, love, and contentment. Our unique ability to choose high or low thoughts—observation deck or gutter—is what makes the human species the most powerful and important of all of God's creations.

We can choose to see ourselves as wonderful, magnificent beings—or not. Very few of us choose to see ourselves as we truly are: wonderful, magnificent manifestations of the Divine One. To rise to and benefit from this high level of thought, you must consciously and conscientiously practice telling yourself how wonderful you are in God.

Why? Because God is in you. We and God are one. God is one in us, meaning God's wholeness, perfection, and completeness are realized (fulfilled) in and through us! When you realize that, and deliberately ponder the wonder and awesomeness of that, you are doing what is known as "practicing the presence of God." You will realize that the phrase "We and God" is more accurately rendered as "We ARE God in expression."

The turtle moves through life with its "house" on its back, even as we move through life with the house of our mind. Unlike the turtle, we can change our house and do it faster!

YOUR "GREEN APPLE" AFFIRMATION #1

Affirmations are mental and verbal *confirmations* of your total and complete belief in your desires, plans, and goals. We enthusiastically encourage you to say your affirmations repeatedly, daily, *and* meditate on them. It will do you so much good to *hear* your affirmations in your own voice. Meditating on them is like wearing a comfortable, warm, and favorite coat: the feeling is so right.

Meditation is spiritual *medication*. It is your Rx for success and can be powerful and instantly effective. The more you meditate on affirmations and say them, the more you SEE them take form and shape in your life. They are your God-given power to create your world as you wish it to be. Do not underestimate their solid, consistent, and reliable universal power. Remember: *FIRM* is a key part of the word *Affirmation*.

And never forget: *it was with the SPOKEN WORD—affirmation—that God created the heavens and the earth.*

Say and see the following Green Apple:

Good flows effortlessly through me. I accept the best that life has to offer. Today, I take a fresh view of life. I am strengthened in my acceptance of the truth that I am one with God, now and forever. I like who and what I am, and I make a commitment to myself today to be good to me. I look for the right instead of the wrong in life today. I give thanks for the increase of understanding that takes place in my life right now. My world is a miracle. I live in the joyous acceptance of this idea. And so it is.

CHAPTER 2

YOUR DIVINITY-IDENTITY

JUST AS IT TAKES physical effort to ascend to the top of the Statue of Liberty, you must have a powerful ambition and overriding desire to get closer to God in order to align yourself with Him. You see, since God is already in you, it is you who must do the moving—in your mind, heart, and spirit. Conscious meditation, daily contemplation, and affirmative prayer are wonderfully efficient and effective means for doing just that.

We can never in reality be disconnected from God. There is only the "appearance" of being disconnected. For, much like gravity, God is everywhere present at all times. The seeming disconnection comes as the result of our giving maximum attention to the "world of appearances" rather than solely to God. Thus we make more powerful and more negative the problem because we do not place our full attention on its answer and solution: God. There is a scripture that says, "We cannot serve God and Mammon." Stated another way, we cannot place our attention on God *and* off God—on something else—at the same time.

DESIGNING YOUR MIND: CASTLE OR CASKET, TOWER OR TOMB?

Your mind, or your consciousness, goes with you wherever you go. Even though you live in a physical dwelling, your mind in reality is your true home. It is always with you. You may leave your residence, which has an address, to work, shop, visit friends, and the like. But you can never leave your mind behind. Therefore, your ability to control the kinds of thoughts you allow into your mind means that you can either free yourself or enslave yourself based on how you think.

Think of it in this way: you can rearrange your home to be beautiful or beauty-less. Would you consider your home to have an attractive interior if you "arranged" your sofa in your kitchen? Your refrigerator in your bedroom? Your stove in your bathroom? Your outside trash containers in your shower? Your "training" and background most assuredly dictate that kitchen appliances are to remain in the kitchen; indeed, they define the kitchen. And other things in your home have their appropriate and exclusive places.

Likewise, it is extremely important that you train the "kitchen" of your mind to contain only those high-quality thoughts that enable you to "cook" on only the first burner. Thoughts are food to the mind. What you think fills your mind just as what you eat fills your stomach. And sooner or later you experience—you see *and* feel—the results. Petty, negative, poisonous thoughts only cause you to experience a petty life filled with grief, frustration, failure, and confusion.

As humans, we are often confused about what really matters. We live in a civilization that puts a premium on looks and appearance. Some people are never quite sure if they look "right," "wrong," or out of place. It is not unusual to see people exploiting every opportunity, even in traffic, to "spruce up" in their car's mirror and make themselves over: some men shave, comb their hair, trim their mustaches; some women brush, apply eyeliner and mascara, or search for blackheads.

Compared to all the attention given to cosmetic details, we leave the mind cluttered, in disarray, and all but abandoned. Though we arrive at our jobs and major appointments presentable, we seldom inquire of ourselves whether our *minds* are presentable. Our face and hair may get "made over" several times a day. However, our mind—rather than being made over—is "done under" by thoughts of anguish, stress, anger, resentment, doubt, fear, and confusion.

Change your mind and KEEP the change!

LIVING LIFE OR LIMITING LIFE

God does not limit us; we limit ourselves. In truth, we are limitless beings, yet we re-define and limit ourselves by convincing ourselves that we cannot accomplish, that we cannot do, that we cannot be. We shackle ourselves inside the prison of our minds. There have been certain individuals throughout the ages who have broken through these shackles and moved into the consciousness of the truth (of our Divine identity).

For example, there was a time when sailors were afraid to sail in their boats outside the confines of the waters around the villages in which they lived. When they looked out at the horizon, where the ocean met the sky, the appearance was that the world was flat. However, there came along an individual named Christopher Columbus, bold enough to move beyond such "flat-minded thinking" and into the reality of limitlessness. His mind became the mental compass that guided him into the discovery of the New World.

For many, many years, athletes who ran the mile event in track-and-field locked and walled themselves inside the belief that no one had the ability to run the mile under 4 minutes. As long as they believed that, every winning runner, with boring repetition, ran a race that was always "4 minutes and something." While track rivals physically bested each other, they just could not defeat their own mental "brainwashing," declaring the impossibility of running a mile under four minutes. Every winning race over four minutes only re-affirmed this very limiting *self-imposed* decree.

Finally in 1956, Roger Bannister, an Englishman, ran the mile in 3 minutes and 59 seconds. The track-and-field world went into an instant uproar. The "impossible" had finally been achieved. Once Roger Bannister broke the 4-minute mile barrier, other athletes realized they could do it too. The news of Bannister's "miracle" transformed runners all over the world, and the mile event was never the same. Milers became known as "clock busters."

Today, running a 4-minute mile is considered "old hat" and unspectacular. Nobody gets excited about it anymore. It's ordinary. Today's world-class miler now occupies a high rank in the "3-minute and something" class. And, unlike generations of runners chained to the 4-minute-mile belief, today's miler has a mind that recognizes absolutely no limits or barriers. He runs his races with the engines of his imagination! At the time this book was being written, teenager Alan Webb, 18 years old, was described in these terms by the nation's press:

The fastest prep miler in U.S. history, after his
3:53.43 mile victory at the May 27, 2001
Prefontaine Classic in Eugene, Oregon, broke
Jim Ryun's 36-year-old record (3:55.3) and
was the fastest U.S. mile in 3 years. (*USA Today*,
June 21, 2001)

As fertilization does to a garden, *imagination* makes us
grow. In order to live a fulfilling, abundant, successful life,
we must *expand* to God, God cannot contract to us. We
cannot contract the Absolute, which is God, but we *can*
expand the relative, which is our own consciousness
(imagination). A great metaphysical teacher, Dr. Eric
Butterworth, advises us that we should have what he calls
the "Ten Golden Minutes." Those are the first ten minutes after we awake each morning, when we do nothing
except expand our consciousness by telling ourselves
how wonderful we are and how wonderful life is. This is
the foundation—the invisible mental, spiritual foundation—that we build and stand upon during the course of
the day.

The story of the three little pigs and the big bad
wolf serves to illustrate that. In that story, the first pig's
house was built of straw, and the big bad wolf came
along and blew his house down. The second little pig's
house was built of wood, and the big bad wolf came
along and blew *his* house down. The third little pig's
house was built of brick, and the big bad wolf came
along and huffed and puffed but he couldn't blow *this*
house down. Its foundation was too strong. The same
applies to consciousness: we must take those golden
minutes, every morning, to create a brick-like, impenetrable consciousness. It is this "fortress" that will pro-

tect us from the negative beliefs and appearances "out there" in the world.

Unfortunately, most people, as the result of the negative experiences they have endured over the years, begin to see their lives as though they were framed in a picture no bigger than a passport photo. It is vital that we enlarge and expand our view of ourselves. This is not something that just happens, but something that we must constantly work at. Just as we brush our teeth, comb our hair, bathe ourselves, and shop for groceries, expanding our view is a lifelong process that we must practice, moment by moment, day by day—indeed, with every breath we take.

> *You can choose to be slave, servant, or lord and master of your own life. What's your choice?*

BELIEF: THE PATH AND POWER TO FREEDOM

Life simply IS. Nothing can be taken from us, in reality, nor can anything be added. God has already made life all that it is supposed to be and filled it with all that it is required to contain. Since life is a state of "is-ness," our mission in life is not to wrestle, worry, wonder, or aimlessly wander. Our role is simply TO BE.

You see, we have a "divinity-identity." We are Divine beings, evolving through—and engaging in—a human experience. Our BEING who we were created to be, and our BELIEVING that we (already) are that, are two powerful "tools" God granted to us *by instilling them in us!* Each time we use these tools, we "realize" (have or become) increasing power, confidence, success. Seeing is believing, *and believing is having.* This means that whatever we desire, we must SEE its fulfillment as already being brought into existence by God through us. Realizing (believing) that law brings our desires into the reality of our experience.

Scientists are aware of hundreds of millions of galaxies and hundreds of millions of stars in each galaxy. There are infinitely more in the universe. And yet we—with a small-mindedness that exerts big control over us—relate primarily to our home, our neighborhood, and the mall. There is so much more (material/substance/life) to us, of which we must be aware: we are part of those galaxies, planets, and those stars. We are made with, of, and from the same "star stuff." We are infinite beings. Everything in the universe has been made for us to have, use, and enjoy.

Humankind is an evolving being whose consciousness cannot remain stagnant, for the nature of the universe is always expanding, moving up, out, and becoming more. There was a time when primitive man dragged his lady around by her hair with one hand and a club in the other, in search of food. Such was the consciousness of the caveman. Today there are pills that you can drop into a container of water; these pills will expand into a full-blown meal for two—you *and* your lady! Fortunately, we have evolved millions of years beyond the caveman era, at least as far as food-gathering goes.

The Wright Brothers created a very primitive machine in the fields of North Carolina that just flew a couple of feet. Today, we have rocket ships and jet planes and spacecraft that go to the outer reaches of the universe. The horse and buggy used to transport people. Today, we have sophisticated automobiles. It is vital for us to realize that we cannot continue to think the same (old) way and make (new) progress in life.

Would we really want to go back to the primitive airplane days of the Wright Brothers? Of course not. We would be embarrassed and frightened to embark on a nonstop flight in the contraptions they invented. Likewise, we have to come out of old ways of thinking and vow never to return to them. It is a contract we must sign with ourselves. We appreciate history's old artifacts, such as primitive airplanes, in museums only. To date, however, we have never seen an airplane fly backward. The point is, we must align ourselves with God and flow *forward* with life itself.

Life is always in a constant state of progression and always advancing. When we experience ups and downs, or when things are slow and life seems to be taking its sweet time, we often shake our heads sadly and declare bitterly, "That's life!" However, it is not life at all. On the contrary, it is we who often want to remain rooted to the spot, stay put, and not move forward. We get comfortable in our routine; we enjoy the groove we've established. Often, a groove becomes a rut, which then becomes a grave. Knowing where we are at any particular time—in a *groove*, a *rut*, or *grave*—helps us to take the necessary steps and keep moving forward and progressing with the flow of life. A Chinese proverb states, "You cannot walk backwards into the future."

Belief requires decision. When you make a decision, all Heaven lines up with you to convert that decision into a real experience.—Tony Buzan, scientist; British Broadcasting Corporation (BBC) producer; author of *Using Both Sides of Your Brain.*

REFUSE TO BE CONFUSED

Our problems in life arise because we think we are left "out there" all by ourselves and are all (or mostly) alone. We spend entire lifetimes behaving as though God has abandoned us, or that earth is an island that we awakened to, after being shipwrecked, battered, and dazed. Nothing could be further from the truth.

Previously, we emphasized the importance of realizing your divinity *with* God. A big step for most, it is nonetheless fundamental—it has to be done—in order to live a full, complete and successful life, one that overflows with abundance in all good things. That is impossible without your realizing and recognizing who you really are. You are not less than God: you *are* God.

The physical body and human form that you claim are you, and upon which you stake your identity, are really only a "space suit," a shell that houses the spirit of God, which lives, moves, and has its being in you. The more you *see* the spirit *in* you, the more the spirit directs your *outer* affairs. This is the simple truth that determines your health, wealth, and happiness. These (and many others) are gifts of the spirit and are yours when you free yourself of the bonds of thinking that you are only a mere mortal—meant to suffer, sacrifice, and sizzle somewhere between heaven and earth. If that's all we are, or were meant to be, God would never have wasted time creating us!

Refuse to be confused by being willing to take charge of your emotions and stand firm in the realization that in some wonderful magnificent, magical, mystical way, we are not apart from God but are a part of God, made in God's image and after God's likeness. If

31

God can't be confused, then neither can we, in reality. Clarity and understanding come by realizing the true nature of our being.

God is always and ever present; it is *we* who often stay stuck in the past or worry about the future. The only definition of time that counts is NOW. That is all we have. That is all we need to have, because *now* is all there is. Our agony and confusion occur when we worry about yesterday, which we cannot bring back, and fret about tomorrow, which we cannot bring forth. So, the result is a wasting of the wonderful moment called "now." While we waste it, God simply waits for us to become aware of Its presence. If it appears to us— as a result of feeling that we're up to our elbows in crocodiles—that God is no longer with us, we must ask ourselves, "Who moved?"

In the heart of a midwestern state is a tourist attraction called the "Talking Rock." An enterprising, energetic businessman had created this one-of-a-kind amusement park for travelers. It was very popular. Among its many wonders was a man-made lake filled with crocodiles. The man took thousands of people to this lake, over a number of years, and always promised $1,000,000 in the form of a cashier's check to anyone who would jump into the lake and swim from one side of it to the other. No one ever challenged him or took him up on his offer. One day, as he was taking a group of tired but excited tourists back to their bus, he stopped at the lake and, as usual, presented them with the $1 million opportunity. And as always, his offer was rejected with a loud "roar" of silence.

But as they turned to make their way to the bus, the tourists heard a loud splash. Turning, they saw a man who had been with their group swimming across the lake for all he was worth. The splashing sound of his arms and legs propelling through the water was punctuated by the thrashing, slapping noise of six huge crocodile tails and six crocodile jaws clamping angrily open and shut.

With all the strength and speed he could muster, he swam toward the shore. It seemed like an eternity to him, but at last he reached it. With less than a half-dozen inches separating his weary legs from the mouths of the six hungry crocodiles, and with his arms numb and his heart hammering inside his chest, he heaved himself out of the water and threw himself onto the bank.

The tourists and the amusement park's owner stood spellbound. Instantly, the owner reached into his coat pocket and pulled out a large envelope. He sprinted over to the man and excitedly thrust the envelope at him. Gulping for air, and with his terror-stricken eyes fixed on the six crocodiles still circling in the lake, he snatched the envelope and hurled it into the lake.

Stunned, the park's owner watched the envelope land in the midst of the crocodiles and exclaimed, "Are you crazy? A million dollars for you was in that envelope! Don't you want it?" Angrily the man breathlessly sputtered, "What [pause] I want is [pause] to know [pause] who pushed me into the water?" Refusing to be confused, he wanted revenge, not reward—something slightly different than what we've been suggesting.

You are made in God's image. I-M-A-G-E means: "I'M Always God Expressed."

WHERE GOD REALLY LIVES

For thousands of years, millions of people have believed and taught others that God lived far off, way up in the sky somewhere, and sat on a throne far beyond the heavens. This notion about God is false and only reinforces an equally false belief that God is remote. Just as illegitimate is the idea that while God takes interest in our human affairs, direct conversations with humans stopped shortly after the last evangelist wrote the last word in the last sentence of the last page of the last book of scripture.

If God does not live somewhere out in the wild blue yonder, then where does God live? And if God is close, does that closeness translate into active interest in our affairs? If God did not stop talking to humans after conversing with the last evangelist, is God then talking with us today? Yes!

You see, God never did cease to be involved or in touch with humans. As we stated earlier, we humans are the ones who moved. Humans, to their own detriment, have concocted the belief that God wants to be as far away from them as possible. As a result, we have concocted the "God-in-the-sky" myth. For most of human history, the concept of a remote God has led to all sorts of superstitions, falsehoods, propaganda, and ignorance about our relationship to God.

The real truth—the whole truth and nothing but the truth—is that God loves us so much, and chose the human being as the "temple" in which to dwell. It is okay to scratch your head a few times, strain your eyes to be sure you read this right, or collapse into a chair and breathe deeply, relieved beyond belief (literally!).

Most people have a distorted view about God. God not only lives in us but is also delighted about being in us. Of all the physical manifestations (e.g. molecules, atoms, planets, wildlife, oceans, fish, fowl, plant life) of God, it is we, the human life-form, who represent MORE of the Divine and eternal essence that is God.

As we are not completely God, nor can we ever be, it is our Divine mission and sole purpose—as humans—to evolve constantly, opening up always to the Divine Presence within, and approaching and seeing and expressing life in the full consciousness of God. In this way, we can remain under the constant direction of the Divine Presence within. Relegated to being humans, we must, and can, ELEVATE to God. Of all the created species, only we—the human species—are able to do this. This, then, is our "mission possible."

Jesus' proclamation about his oneness with God was also declaring Jesus' express desire for us to declare that exact same truth: we and the Father are one. However, instead of declaring that, we do just the opposite. We limit our relationship with God by denying the very relationship ordained and established with and for us! Countless religious dogmas have been created and, throughout millennia, numberless human beings have devoted their entire lives insisting that Jesus' words pertained only to himself and nobody else.

We have totally misrepresented Jesus' role and work. He was an example of a human being living and loving and working as God. He was showing us that we too were created to live and love and work as God. Perhaps the greatest injury organized religion has done to its various followers is teaching them to refuse to accept the greatest gift God gave us: Divine Presence right inside us. Religion, then, is driven by the opinions and views of humans, not of God. Religion is not holy, it is merely restrictive. And in its wholesale misinterpretation of Jesus' vital words, it has even been repressive of those who see the light and proclaim, "I and my father are one."

Jesus' work on earth was to convince humanity of its divinity—not convert anybody to anything.

Freedom from Humanity's Insanity

You see, Jesus came into the world not to save it but to FREE it from the false beliefs and teachings of humankind. Rather than teach people to live a Christ-like life, filled with miracles every day, religion has taught that miracles occur only rarely and that one's reward in life is pain and punishment and struggle rather than hope and glory. Human beings, for thousands of years, have been programmed to believe this.

Let us analyze the word *religion* to understand the incredible physical and mental cruelties, as well as spiritual harm, the word itself has historically represented. *Religare,* in Latin, means "to tie back." Think of how your ligaments tie muscle back to or around bone, and how the ligature on a clarinet or saxophone ties the reed back around the mouthpiece. *Re,* in the Latin, also specifically means to do something again or repeatedly. For example, *review* means "to look at again." Thus, *re-ligare* means "to tie back again," that is, "to re-tie." *Gion* means a developed system or accumulation of something. For example, *region* means an accumulation of land or area, or a systemic sphere such as an ocean.

The word *religion* had awful significance in ancient times and in the Old World, when The Church (emphasis intended) had unlimited and ultimate authority, set forth the laws, and often regularly unleashed its abusive power upon its fear-riddled believers with deadly sanctions enforced by the state. Frequently, the Church and the state were joint partners in controlling and persecuting the people. The mass citizenry's fear and resentment of their lives being hurled back and forth, trapped between the Church and the state in a crushing double bind, can clearly be seen in the full meaning of the word *religion:* a system of control to tie back again—between Church and state.

When the founders of America created the nation's laws, "freedom of religion" became both the national cry and a vehement denunciation of the Church of old. However, this phrase is an inadvertent oxymoron that means free to choose how one wishes to be tied back again! Residing deep in the hearts of many Americans was another obsession: freedom FROM religion. As part of the christening of the New World, America's founders quickly drew up and ratified legislation mandating the separation of church and state.

It is advisable that you not get into an argument about religion with anybody. Human beings historically have exacted cruel penalties for the mere utterance of the words "I and my Father are one." In spite of the absolute truth of those words, Jesus' experience is only one of many that show us what can lie in store for someone stating that truth. Simply demonstrating good in all aspects of your life and doing good to others is the best and most obvious example of God working in and through you that you can provide.

God lives in you. That's the reason the Great Example—Jesus—who lived 2,000 years ago said, "I and my father are one." We are supposed to declare that same proclamation and believe and live it. And, in the greatest prayer ever uttered, Jesus began it by saying, "Our Father..." because he knew that the Source of his life was the Source of all life—yours and mine included. In many churches and other religious institutions you'll find pictures of Jesus looking up toward the sky with the appearance of a light beaming down on him. However, in reality, the light is coming from within his soul, and it represents love, peace, harmony, truth, and beauty, *which each individual has the ability to express.*

When the writers of the scriptures spoke of the light, they were not alluding to the kinds of light that we are aware of and use today—light bulbs in our homes, streetlights, and even starlight. They were talking about *inner* illumination, the individual's consciousness being filled with the light of truth regarding one's being and oneself as one relates to the whole of life. And the Great Teacher Jesus directed you and me to "Let your light so shine...." The same light that shone through Jesus can shine through us. It is the *identical* light that Jesus' father—our father—created and placed *inside* us.

Live from the consciousness of God. That means live with an intimate link to God, a star-high awareness of Its presence and power in your life, and a complete sense and knowingness that God is "online" (in you and for you) all the time. As Betty Eadie states in her wonderful book *Embraced by the Light*, we must talk to God, think about God, listen to God many times every day. We must be consumed by the consciousness of God just as we are *fully* involved with breathing: automatically and all the time. Know and recognize that God's space is your place.

Know and feel God in every muscle of your body; in every blink of your eye; in every swallow of food you take; in every act of love you express; in every word you utter; in every child you teach; in every thought you think; and every time you are in the presence of another human being. Place God in every business transaction you make. Thank God for every circumstance or experience in which you are involved. Talk to God from the time you arise each morning to the time you retire each night. This can be in the form of silent prayer or verbalized utterances. What we are encouraging you to do is improve and enhance your life by using maximum energy (prayer and meditation) to recognize, accept, and bond with your Creator God, and thankfully and with great joy confirm your Divinity-Identity.

My congregation and I adore a song entitled "I Love Myself." We sing it every week. Written by Mr. Jai Joseph, it really speaks to the high regard in which we ought to hold ourselves at all times. Let's look at the verses of this wonderful song and feel its almost magical beauty, power, and—most of all—meaning:

> *I love myself the way I am, there's nothing I need to*
> * change.*
> *I'll always be the perfect me, there's nothing to rearrange.*
> *I'm beautiful and capable of being the best me I can.*
> *And I love myself just the way I am.*
> *I love you just the way you are. There's nothing you*
> *need to do.*

*When I feel the love inside myself, it's easy to love
you.*
*Behind your fears, your rage and tears, I see your
shining star.*
And I love you just the way you are.
I love the world just the way it is, 'cause I can clearly see
*That all things I judge are done by people just like
me.*
*So 'til the birth of peace on earth that only love can
bring*
I'll help it grow by loving everything,
I love myself the way I am and still I want to grow.
*But change outside can only come when deep inside
I know*
I'm beautiful and capable of being the best me I can.
And I love myself just the way I am,
I love myself just the way I am.

If you were to pass by an apple tree and the apples
had the ability to talk, they would perhaps say to you,
"I, apple tree, am God, expressing Itself by means of
me." In like manner, it is necessary that we come to a
place in consciousness where we realize that we are
much like the apple and God is much like the tree—
the substance and source of our being. Therefore it is
necessary that we remind ourselves constantly of this
reality.

There is one mind, one life, one love, one presence,
one joy that is one God, eternally expressing itself by
means of Its creation. Our responsibility to ourselves is
to mentally turn away from the world of events and
effects, situations and circumstances, and all distracting
situations, and contemplate the true essence of our

being. We must mentally grasp a sense of oneness with our Source.

> *Say to yourself, many times a day, "I [your name] am God expressing Itself as me—God's means." Or, "I [your name] am the body of God, and God, my Creator, is delighted to have Its home in me."*

DECISIONS, LIKE INCISIONS, ARE SHARP AND POTENT

Decisions build worlds. You MUST make a decision. The famous New York Yankees catcher and homespun philosopher Yogi Berra said, "If you see a fork in the road, take it." In other words, make some kind of a decision! Standing in the *middle* of the road is dangerous. You will get knocked down by the traffic coming at you from both directions!

When climbing a ladder, in order to reach for the (success) rung above, it is absolutely necessary that we release the rung below. Even a turtle, in order to make progress, has to *decide* to stick its neck out. You are responsible for what is in your life. If you've got it, you brought it. The mind is like a magnet. It draws to us what we give our attention to. What you give your attention to *attends*—comes, or returns—to you.

As an entertainer I traveled to Australia frequently, and I have many friends who are Aborigines. The first time I met some of my friends who lived in the city, they carried me to the Outback, where they lived originally, to introduce me to their families and their way of life. One of my friends gave me a boomerang and asked me to throw it. He also, in the same breath, suggested that after I throw it, I should do one of two things: catch it or duck. He knew all too well that it was coming back from its point of departure. Life is much like that boomerang. What you give it, in terms of your thought process, it gives back—*boomerangs*—to you in abundance. So make certain that the thoughts you give to life are something you'd truly like to experience.

Change your life by changing your thinking. The apostle Paul, who was a prolific thinker and writer, said, "Be ye transformed by the renewing of your mind." In modern terminology, we might translate that to mean: "Your life will change when you change the way you think about life." There is not now, nor has there ever been, nor will there ever be, a lack of any good thing in this universe. There has never been a cosmic famine. To even consider or suggest such an event is to insult God. God's goodness, grace, and beauty cannot be exhausted. Everything that God is, is eternal—forever! And that includes you! There is an abundance of every good thing on this earth plane.

In our desire to wield power and control, we create the appearance of lack and limitation. Economic upheavals, food shortages, and wars all play a role in producing this gross distortion. Likewise, we can create peace and prosperity simply by *deciding* that they must be the gifts every single human being should possess. That's right! If we truly desire peace, prosperity, and abundance in every good thing, we can have them all.

Your experience is an expression and production of your thinking.

YOUR "GREEN APPLE" AFFIRMATION #2

Affirmations are mental and verbal *confirmations* of your total and complete belief in your desires, plans, and goals. We enthusiastically encourage you to say your affirmations repeatedly, daily, *and* meditate on them. It will do you so much good to *hear* your affirmations in your own voice. Meditating on them is like wearing a comfortable, warm, and favorite coat: the feeling is so right.

Meditation is spiritual *medication*. It is your Rx for success and can be powerful and instantly effective. The more you meditate on affirmations and say them, the more you SEE them take form and shape in your life. They are your God-given power to create your world as you wish it to be. Do not underestimate their solid, consistent, and reliable universal power. Remember: *FIRM* is a key part of the word *Affirmation*.

And never forget: *it was with the SPOKEN WORD—affirmation—that God created the heavens and the earth.*

Say and see the following Green Apple:

Today I trust in Divine Guidance. I rely upon GOD's WISDOM to make straight my way, perfecting and harmonizing every situation in my life. My belief is in this Divine security, and I know that all is not only well with me and my affairs, but is also well with those with whom I associate. The everlasting arms support and sustain each of us, perfectly. And so it is.

CHAPTER 3

PRAYER AND MEDITATION: YOUR INSTANT, CONSTANT POWER

WE BELIEVE THAT MEDITATION is spiritual *medication*. In order to live the God-intended life, it is necessary that we take it upon ourselves to work on ourselves. You need to give yourself a specified amount of time, as soon as you awaken in the morning, to build a spiritual platform upon which you stand that day. You are the only one who can build the platform and high observation tower you need to surmount the mountain of obstacles and confront the adversities the world of appearances and events produces.

Construction of this platform can be done only through meditation and affirmative prayer, contemplating and gratefully accepting the goodness of life. The Great Teacher Jesus said, "Pray [affirmatively] without ceasing." It is constant prayer that makes and keeps strong the planks in the platform of your observation tower. If you cease to pray, then you *see* the problems with which the world of appearances and events "greets" you. And that which you constantly see will *seize* you.

45

What, exactly, does prayer do? What it does *not* do is change God's mind. Prayer changes the mind, the outlook, the attitude of the one who is praying, the one seeking the answer, the one in need of the healing. That is the whole point of prayer—to change our mind and bring us into *alignment* with the Mind of God—in line with THE mind. Our prayer should always be on the affirmative side of life. Our prayers should be stated as affirmative truths. When we meditate, we should always be in a listening mode, listening to the imparting of the intuitive guidance from the Source of our life, *which is within us.*

We might conceive of prayer as working out or attacking a "problem" in this way:

P	R	O	B	L	E	M
r	o	u	a	i	t	i
a	o	t	r	n	e	n
y	t		r	k	r	d
e	s		r	s	r	
r			i		n	
			e		a	
			r		l	
			s			

Moreover, prayer can be seen as: *P–ositive R–esource A–lways Y–ielding E–ternity's R–esponse.* As Dr. Barbara King, author of the book *Transform Your Life*, says in her public pronouncements, "Be the prayer that you pray."

Our obsession with our wants and our needs is caused by a panicked sense of separation from our good. As a consequence, there always seem to be chaos and confusion in the world; it also seems as though life is only a constant struggle to meet our needs. We look out at the world of events and effects and we deem it to be the reality. Our fear of and paranoia about life are the result of the "separation-anxiety" neurosis within our own minds.

When I do workshops, I hand out a form to all of the participants on which are listed six of life's "vital areas": Health, Prosperity, Relationships, Employment, Social Life, and Peace of Mind. Participants are instructed to cross out, with an "X," the area most frequently absent or deficient. Regardless of the number of other boxes that are also crossed out, "Peace of Mind" is always ranked by participants as the prime component most difficult to find.

The purpose of this workshop is to enable participants to realize that they are made in the image and likeness of God. If God is peace, and if they choose to recognize their oneness with God, it is in that recognition that they begin to find peace for themselves. Despite its apparent simplicity, this is not a casual or insignificant process. It is serious, powerful, and requires dedication and an attitude of sincere searching.

It takes some persons longer than others to realize their oneness—indeed, sameness—with God. The purpose of this book is to save you time and heartache as you seek to better understand your *heritage* with your Creator. It should not take you the rest of your life to realize your Divinity-Identity! For some people, that is *exactly* what happens; for others, the realization *never* seems to come.

The more you express God, the more you experience good.

STUDY: IT MAKES YOU READY

Sincere, dedicated and regular study is the surest, most efficient way to knowledge for increasing your good. The majority of people desire having their lives changed. However, many do not want to do anything to change them. It has been said that one definition of insanity is doing the same thing over and over and expecting a different result.

It is important that we study the wisdom of the ages, but it is infinitely more important that we put into action—in our daily living—what we study. There is a biblical passage that states, "Faith without works is dead," meaning that when you don't put faith into action—you merely *have* it. Like a trophy, it just sits somewhere on your mental shelf inactive, immobile, frozen.

> *The more you study, the more you learn. The more you learn, the more you know. Life is the ultimate "knowledge game."*

GIVING: THE SECRET TO A THRIVING LIFE

Lack and limitation come from not having a *giving* consciousness. God is a *giving* God. But we live in a *get* society, and the behavior of getting, of acquiring, often overtakes our inherent spiritual purpose of *giving*. In life, there are only two kinds of people. They are not black or white, brown or yellow, Christian or Jew, Buddhist or Hindu, Muslim or Sikh, Democrat or Republican. They are *givers* and *takers*. And since this is a Universe that always gives, and never takes, it is necessary that we wise up and live in harmony with it. Plant an apple seed and the earth gives you an entire tree—an apple tree, filled with an abundance of apples that are filled with enough seeds to reproduce acres of apple orchards. And so the creative process goes on endlessly, because it is life itself.

It is the law of the Universe that as you give, so you receive. We choose the amount of good that the Universe gives to us. For example, we can chose to take a thimble to a great body of water and submerge it, and the water will fill it. We can do the same with a cup, a drinking glass, a bucket, a No. 10 washtub, or the *Titanic*. The body of water—the ocean—will fill whatever receptacle we place in it. As a matter of fact, there does not exist a physical container so large that an oceanic body of water cannot fill it.

Spiritually speaking, our receptacle is our consciousness. The Universe is the body of water. God does not resist us. Our problems occur as a result of our limited, diminutive consciousness. That is the reason the Great Teacher Jesus said, "It is done unto you as you believe." You see, we are constantly giving, whether we know it or not. What we receive is equal to what we have given—in thought or action. The Universe gives back to us through the same size hole through which we give. That is why the scriptures tell us, "The liberal [generous] soul shall be made fat [wealthy]." God deliberately created us with the ability to expand our consciousness and thus fulfill (achieve) the scriptures' proclamation (prediction) for and about us!

You can participate fully in life's creative process and realize unlimited good.

GOD IS A GIVING GOD

There is a beautiful story in the scripture that is allegorical, very profound, and that relates to our grasping the nature of God. One night in a dream, the story goes, God came to King Solomon and told him he would grant his one desire. Whatever his desire was, he could name it, but it could be only one thing.

The majority of us might have asked for greater wealth, a better job, or a physical body expressing perfect health—all things of a material nature. But King Solomon, being a very wise and humble man, said, "The one thing I would like more than any other is wisdom and understanding."

We, like King Solomon, if we are to live the God-intended life, must understand our relationship to God. To realize that God is a *giving* God, all we need do is to look around us and see the infinite number of expressions of beauty and goodness that have been bestowed upon us. The Great Teacher Jesus admonished us to be perfect even as our Father in heaven is perfect. You see, our Source *is* perfect. So we are to express (our Source's) perfection to as great a degree as we possibly can in the manner in which we live our lives.

Jesus also said, "When you see me, you've seen the Father." Or, expressed another way, he was simply saying, "When you see me, you're seeing the most perfect and complete example of life, in its wondrousness and magnificence, being expressed through a human form. He also said, "The things I have done you can do also." He was always putting life's "ball" in our hands (to use a sports analogy) because he realized that it truly was (and will always be) our "play," or responsibility, to become aware of our relationship, our oneness, with God.

Unless and until we accept this truth, we cannot achieve success in life and experience the abundant and unlimited good that God has already ordained for us. Though we are made as humans, to better fulfill our roles on this earth we must always remind ourselves of the scriptural proclamation that we are in fact made in the "image and likeness" of God. That declaration is powerful evidence of who and what we really are.

Just as we can see our reflection (image) in a mirror, and we may occasionally use a photograph of ourselves to establish a "positive I.D." (likeness), God sees us as spirit-filled beings—we are human photographs of God's "image and likeness"—constantly evolving in our spiritual development to do—as Jesus did—"the will of the Father." As impossible as it is to look in a mirror and see somebody else instead of ourselves, it is equally and infinitely possible to be, do, and have absolutely everything we desire by first understanding that we are made in the image and likeness of God, and therefore accepting our oneness with our Creator.

Look around you and count all your good. It will take forever but it will sure improve your eyesight!

IT'S ALL GOD . . . BUT WHAT IS THE "STUFF" OF GOD?

Another way of looking at this is to consider that the wave is one with the ocean, the ray of the sun is one with the sun. *We are God in human form.* We all are "rays" of, and from, God. The God that we are is *spirit*—it indwells the body. Our body in and of itself has no power. The body does not decide to go to the grocery store or on vacation—or to do anything, for that matter.

There is something unseen in the body, and yet eternally powerful, that causes it to do what it does. This unseen something is spirit, life, the soul of the universe, expressing itself. The body, much like our automobile, is a vehicle. The body cannot operate without us (the spirit) inside.

This vehicle called the body transports the spirit, which tells it where to go and what to do—just as we "tell" (by driving) our autos where to go and what to do. Therefore, we are not human beings having a spiritual experience. Rather, *we are spiritual beings having a human experience.* We are God in physical, human expression.

Quite frankly, however, for the majority of people that truth is inconceivable. They just cannot understand it, they will not have it, and therefore they reject it, as though it were totally false, like some fabricated fiction. Unable to accept this truth, they subsequently find their lives to be a constant and unwelcome struggle. Blind to (or in denial about) their own role in producing their negative, unfruitful or failing lives, most people live these lives (as Thoreau put it) "in quiet desperation."

Such persons are only partially to blame, however. In most religions, simply thinking that you are something more than a mere human being is considered sinful. Humans have even created sinister and ominous-sounding words to warn about, identify, and condemn such thinking: *heresy, apostasy, blasphemy.*

I have an automobile with customized license plates. I submitted a request to the state Department of

MotorVehicles for them and completed all the required paperwork. It took the agency more than 3 months to make a decision whether to grant my request for these "unusual" license plates. Finally, I received them. I still own that automobile, and it still carries those plates. Here is what they say to one and all within visual range: U R G O D.

Whenever I park this car and leave it somewhere, I am almost always greeted on my return with hand-scribbled notes plastered all over the car's windshield. Most of these communications are not flattering! On the contrary, they are negative, accusatory, and might even be considered offensive. However, I do not allow myself to be offended. And I am indeed blessed and grateful that both my car and its attention-getting license plates have, to date, remained intact, undamaged, and unblemished. I sincerely believe that people who become annoyed by these plates but are sufficiently able to confine their annoyance to writing their thoughts on paper and presenting them to me on my windshield...well, they are good, well-intentioned persons in their hearts.

You see, everything, everywhere, is God in expression—even those experiences and circumstances that we believe are not, because of their origins or effects upon us. Since God is omnipresent, omnipotent, and omniscient, then God has to be everywhere and in everything, all the time. Our good friend, Dr. Linda Logan, tells a beautiful story of a farmer who had two small boys, 5 and 6 years old. Both wanted a horse for Christmas. On Christmas Eve, they were restless and could hardly sleep, they were so excited. Finally, they drifted off to sleep and on Christmas morning they ran to their father and insisted that he immediately take them to "our horses." He led them outside to a pile of horse manure alongside the barn.

The pile looked almost as large as the barn itself. The father handed each boy a shovel and told them that if they wanted to know whether or not they had a horse, they would have to begin digging through the pile of horse manure. The first little boy took a few hesitant steps forward, shook his head, backed up, and returned his shovel to his dad, saying, "I'll take a bicycle and some skates instead."

His brother said, "I'll do it, Dad. Give me the shovel!" His father asked him why he would want to do all that dirty work. "Wouldn't you just rather have a bicycle and some skates, like your brother?" he asked. The boy stood tall and shook his head with determination. "Absolutely not, Dad," he replied. "From the size of that pile of manure, I know there's got to be a pony in there somewhere!"

We all encounter difficulties and problems. Occasionally, life—with or without horses!—seems to be a huge and smelly burden. But through it all, we have got to be willing to dig through life's negative and unsightly appearances, and especially through our own mental and emotional "pile." (What's stinking is our own thinking.) And as we dig and dig and dig some more, we have to realize and know that God is there. All that digging is for building your faith muscle.

Life is for you and always provides the answers you need.

Giving and Receiving Are the Same Thing

It is absolutely impossible to give without receiving—
because, as we noted earlier, that is the law and nature
of the Universe. Evidence of that fairly shouts at us
everywhere we turn. The abundant flowers and trees
are the result of someone's giving a seed to the earth of
the very same kind. The earth gives back the exact likeness of that which we give it. Again, that is the
Universe's law.

In fact, if we look at nature at work, we see the law
of the Universe in action. What, then, is the Universe
telling us about giving and receiving? We are always
receiving through the same size hole that we give.
Why? Because in reality, we are never *giving*. Instead, *we
are creating the consciousness by which the universe gives
through us.*

An example from plumbing might serve to illustrate
this. The more you open a water faucet, the more
water comes through. As you begin to shut it, the less
water comes through the faucet. The same principle
applies to giving and receiving. The more your consciousness is open to giving, the more the Universe
gives through your consciousness. How much or how
little you receive—in peace, happiness, love, kindness,
or material things—depends on how open or shut your
consciousness is.

Big givers are big receivers—in *all* things, not just
material goods. As we observed earlier, the scripture
states: "The liberal soul shall be made fat." If you are
dissatisfied with the amount of money in your bank
account and the quality and quantity of your material
goods, examine the size of the hole through which you

give. Is it big or small? Do you give frequently or only occasionally? How and what you give is how and what you will receive.

There was once a man who went to the "traditional" hell, and there he saw tormented, wasted, emaciated, and desperate-looking people seated at—a banquet! An especially hair-raising sight was how grotesque they looked with spoons tied to their hands—spoons that were too long for them to feed themselves with. He grew sickened at the sight of watching their feeble and futile attempts to eat the sumptuous meal.

Unable any longer to take in the horrifying sight, the man decided to leave hell and visit the "traditional" heaven. There, he found happy people with robust and healthy bodies seated before a comparable feast. He could not help noticing the kinds of spoons they used to feed themselves. The spoons were the exact size, kind, and length used by those tortured people whom he had just seen in hell.

Despite the oddly-long handles on their spoons, these people in heaven appeared very content. In fact, he was greeted loudly and enthusiastically and invited to "sit and sup" with a group who were laughing, singing, and chattering among themselves as they ate and drank with vigor.

The man looked from left to right, trying to figure out the difference between the group he had seen in hell and the group whom he was now visiting in heaven. A tap on his shoulder interrupted his thoughts. Frowning, he turned to see who beckoned and simultaneously *saw* the answer to his nagging question: an outstretched spoon, filled with the rich aroma of a fine soup, waited inches from his own lips.

Holding the spoon was a woman whose face radiated love, kindness, and joy. As though he had just awakened, his head snapped up and his frown disappeared. He
waved his hands excitedly in the air, for he now had the
answer: *the people in heaven were feeding each other!* That is,
they were *giving* and *receiving* from each other—the
grandest and most gracious gesture of helpfulness and
support.

The people in hell were selfish, trying only to keep
their *individual* bodies and souls together. The people in
heaven were selfless, thinking *first* of giving, to render aid
and assistance to somebody else. As a result, they were
always rewarded in turn. Their giving made them *eligible*
to receive. These liberal souls were well fed, happy, and
healthy. They were guaranteed a permanent place in
heaven's "receiving line."

The world of events and effects has conditioned us to
think that when we give, we will have *less than we had* or
nothing at all. But precisely the opposite is the case. The
more we give, the more the Universe ensures that we
have. Because the Universe always ensures that we have
something to give. We can never out-give the Universe,
and therefore we can never out-give ourselves.

This is the backbone of the principle of tithing. It is
not so much a physical process as it is a spiritual law.
When we tithe, we are following the scripture that says,
"Give and it shall be given unto you, pressed down, shak-
en together and running over." Tithing is our acknowledgment and verification to the Universe that we trust
the Universe. Our acts of tithing tell the Universe that we
are not apart *from* it but a part *of* it. This is especially
understood in the powerful scriptural declaration: "Bring
all the tithes into the storehouse...I will open up the

windows of heaven for you and pour out a blessing so great you won't have room enough to take it in!"

Whenever lack and limitation seem to crowd you out, tithe...and you'll soon have something to shout about.

Tithing: Your Key to the Universe's Treasures

Suppose you were to take a pie and cut it into six equal slices, each slice representing a phase of life (relationships, employment, health, tithing). If one *slice* of the pie is removed, the pie is no longer *whole.* The same principle applies to our livingness. For example, if you were to take the tithing slice out of your life's pie, you would no longer be whole. Your life would not be complete. There would be a constant, chronic nagging feeling that something was missing. Regular, consistent tithing guarantees that you will have a good, joyous, and abundant life in *all* areas, not just financial.

Contrary to popular belief, you don't *get* money; you *release* it and it returns to you. Many people think they *make* money, but the United States Mint does that for us. What we give to the Universe—as a release—returns back to us in the manner and form in which we give.

A dear friend of ours, Janet Clark, was teaching a prosperity-consciousness class to some beautiful people who happened to live in a low-income area. One night there were about 30 participants in Ms. Clark's class. After introductions, she formed them into a circle and asked them to close their eyes and imagine that they were sitting atop and sinking into an ever-growing mountain of money.

She told them that, in addition to visualizing this great wealth, they had to *feel* its abundance, take it up in their hands, play in it, even bathe in it, and use it for their own and others' good. "Be joyful with your wealth, toss it up in the air and over your heads. Start getting used to an endless supply of money from your Eternal Source."

Most of the participants obediently and immediately got caught up in the vivid scenes they created in their minds. By their ecstatic expressions, it was clear they enjoyed surrounding and immersing themselves in lavish and abundant monetary wealth. It was also clear that sitting atop their imaginary mountain of money was something they would have enjoyed doing all night long. Their minds were sharp, active, and they used them that night to the fullest, in mentally and enthusiastically creating their overflowing wealth.

However, not everyone appeared joyful or even fully involved in the activity. One person constantly frowned as though angry or injured. Deep lines of intense pain formed in her face. When Ms. Clark concluded the activity, she could hardly wait to ask this obviously uncomfortable person why she had not seemed to enjoy playing in her "money mountain" as had the other participants. She asked her why she seemed to be uncomfortable and in obvious pain.

Without hesitation, the woman replied, "All of those hard pennies falling onto my head were giving me knots and a headache!" What you give out to the Universe you get back, in the exact form and manner in which you gave it. This woman's experience demonstrates a powerful truth, one that we can not afford to overlook: the less you give, the less you get back—and the more painful the "return" is!

The Bank of Life always accepts your "thought deposits" and pays you interest rates according to the level of your consciousness.

IF YOU WAIT, YOU WANT

Don't wait for your ship to come in—go out and meet it. Develop a plan and get busy making it a reality. The most important part of this activity must take place in your own mind. You must not wait—in fact, why should you?—when your good is already here. Your ship has already arrived long ago! The goods "on board" are instantly and always available to you.

To wait for our ship to come in—a cliché whose utterance should be questioned but seldom is—is to put a *weight* on ourselves when there is no need to do so. Would you continue to "wait" for an important letter or other correspondence that had *already* arrived in your mailbox? Of course not. Then you must realize that your *acceptance* of God's good for you is all that is necessary to receive and benefit from it. Accepting it—and doing so with thanksgiving—must be as automatic and as constant as breathing.

There is a scripture that directs us to "Be still and know that I am God." However, that was never intended to mean that one is to physically sit and do nothing. Idleness seems to be the favorite activity of those who "wait"—for whatever it is they are awaiting. The stillness spoken of is not the act of *sitting still*, but rather the discipline of *quieting the thoughts* that race through the mind.

Use the energy from those thoughts—line them up, so to speak—to form a picture of what you desire to be, to have, or to experience. Then proceed to do what is necessary to bring the picture in your mind into objective form and vivid reality.

When you take a roll of film to a photo lab and later return to pick up the developed prints, suppose you spot a photo of yourself that you do not like. You decide to tell the lab person that you are not pleased with that particular photo, and you ask him to print another photo from the *same* negative. You return an hour later and find that you have the exact same print, just as before. Absolutely nothing in the photograph has changed.

If you want the print to change, you've got to change the *negative*. If we want our life's experiences to change, we've got to change the (negative) image of life that we have in our mind, upgrade and elevate it, and then watch the desired picture develop.

Isn't it interesting that photographs are developed from things called *negatives?* More than a mere coincidence, here is the lesson this teaches us: keep the same negative and you keep the same picture of your life. *Change* the negative—stinking thinking in all its forms and behaviors—and you change the entire picture of your life. It is *always* in your power to change the negatives in your life and produce radiant and stunning and flattering pictures.

"Picture perfect" is a term meant to describe you and everything else about you!

THE PLAY CALLED LIFE: STAGED IN THE THEATER OF YOUR MIND

"Mind over matter" is more than a cliché. Correctly understood, it means that mind is all; it is everything. What occurs or develops in the mind will eventually be seen and felt in our outer experiences (matter). Mind *produces* matter and mind *prevails* over matter. So what develops in the mind is *all* that "matters"!

In this play called life, the set design, the script, and the characters and their actions are all developed in the theater of your mind. Without ever working in the stage or screen industry, you are involved in "live" theater every day of your life. Indeed, you are the *producer*. If you do not like your productions, you can change them, just as a choreographer changes her dance numbers, a band leader his arrangements, a singer her repertoire.

But first you must recognize that it all begins in the mind. What you think, you eventually *see* as circumstance. What you express in mind, you *get* as experience. As a carpenter builds a house from blueprints, it is your mind that builds—from your own "thought-prints"—the *structure* of your experience.

An eastern university decided to devote six months to testing whether or not intercollegiate basketball players would alter the way they were playing the game by engaging in an experiment involving an "alternative" method of practicing and playing. Three groups of ten players of equal ability were chosen for this experiment.

The first group showed up at the basketball court daily and shot free throws and played for an hour. The second group did not go anywhere; they stayed in their room and, for an hour each day, *imagined* themselves shooting free throws and playing. The third group did absolutely nothing; during the six-month duration of the experiment, they did not even touch a basketball or venture near a court.

At the end of the six-month period, the university brought all the players together for a game of basketball and analyzed their play. As might have been expected, the third group was "rusty," their timing was off, and they played an incompetent, lackluster game. Equally expected was the first group's results. They played just as if they had been practicing (of course, they had) and won their game handily.

But it was the results of the second group that stunned everybody. Though away from the basketball court and even a basketball for 180 days (six months), they played the game as though they had never been away from it. And, indeed, they had not: *they had been playing it every day, for an hour, in their minds.* Their winning results and point totals were equal to those of the first group—the only group that had been actually playing the game every day for six months.

Your mind is the best field or court upon which to play whatever game Life presents to you.

WHATEVER YOU WANT, *GIVE* IT FIRST

The great Chinese philosopher Confucius has been quoted as having said, "The journey of 1,000 miles begins with the first step." It is we who must take the first step toward whatever we want in life. Most people would be surprised to know what the first step *must* be: *give first that which you wish to receive.* Whatever you want in life, you must give it first. If you want love, then give love; if happiness, make someone happy. Expand your life in the direction you want it to go by first giving in that direction.

The great emperor Napoleon thought big, he thought grand. He saw everything on a large scale. Yet in physical stature he was a very small man—less than 5 feet tall. But when you see pictures of him sitting astride a horse, his legs hang below the stomach of the horse—giving the appearance of regal stature. In reality, his feet could not reach the middle of the saddle—that's how diminutive in height he was. Yet even in the smaller details of his life he thought big and used his mind to open up and expand opportunities in the direction in which he wanted to go. Likewise, we must expand our view of ourselves in terms of connecting and giving to life. When we give to life and to each other on a grand scale, it is we who become the beneficiaries.

Your mind is connected directly to the Universe to fulfill all your needs.

YOUR "GREEN APPLE" AFFIRMATION #3

Affirmations are mental and verbal *confirmations* of your total and complete belief in your desires, plans, and goals. We enthusiastically encourage you to say your affirmations repeatedly, daily, *and* meditate on them. It will do you so much good to *hear* your affirmations in your own voice. Meditating on them is like wearing a comfortable, warm, and favorite coat: the feeling is so right.

Meditation is spiritual *medication*. It is your Rx for success and can be powerful and instantly effective. The more you meditate on affirmations and say them, the more you SEE them take form and shape in your life. They are your God-given power to create your world as you wish it to be. Do not underestimate their solid, consistent, and reliable universal power. Remember: *FIRM* is a key part of the word *Affirmation*.

And never forget: *it was with the SPOKEN WORD— affirmation—that God created the heavens and the earth.*

Say and see the following Green Apple:

My faith is based on an inner conviction, not upon an outer circumstance. I believe in God. I believe in myself. I am guided, guarded, and protected by the Spirit that dwells within me. Wherever I go, God gets there first. Each day provides me with an opportunity to take charge of my thoughts, my feelings, my actions, and my beliefs. Knowing this is the day that God has made, I rejoice in it. Regardless of what happens today, I remain calm because that is the habit I choose to form. I move through each day with dignity. I know what to say and how to say it. I affirm that only good goes from me, and good—and good alone— returns to me. For this I am grateful. And so it is.

CHAPTER 4

LIVING IN THE WINNER'S CIRCLE

A WINNER IS a person who realizes that he or she has activated God or good in some way, or through some means, in his/her life. An extremely important concept that few realize or believe is that *anybody* can be a winner, although not everybody is. It is a fact that winning in the overall "game" of life does not require that you first have to be rich, famous, fast, strong, big, tall, of a certain racial background, or of genius intelligence.

However, winning does require that once you make a *commitment* to be a winner, you stay *focused* on attaining your desired goal. Occasional obstacles that knock you off your feet are nothing compared to the immeasurable unhappiness and deep sense of failure that often result from giving up on or getting sidetracked from the goal. To arrive at the finish line at the end of your "race," you have to *finish* the race—that is why it is called the "finish line."

> *Life is meant to be lived fully, not partially. Winning can only be complete; there is no such thing as a partial victory.*

Playing the Game of Life

The game of life is remarkably like an athletic game. The number of boxers, tennis players, runners, baseball players, and swimmers enshrined by the press and idolized by their adoring publics for their incredible physical skills are merely a fraction of countless other athletes who toil at these sports but fail to become world-class champions. You see, the champions of every sport have been knocked down, hurt, locked in a slump and made to sit on the bench just as the non-champions have.

What is the defining difference between champions and non-champions? There is something in champions that will not allow them to remain prone on the canvas, rooted on the sidelines, or encased on the bench. Although the often equal skills of champions and non-champions bring them together and would appear to make them equivalent in potential, skill alone does not make them equal. The difference between champions and non-champions—the difference that separates their worlds—is the *quality and state of their minds.*

You can win at the game of life—and only if you decide to play like a champion.

Inside the Mind of the Champion

The champion has the mind of a *winner.* And the winner's mind is filled with a firm, unshakable belief in good. A winner leaves no room for doubt. Doubt to a winner is like what being out of condition is to an athlete—a real handicap. The winner stays in condition by *staying* with this belief.

In order to achieve good, one's mind has to be free of any encumbrances: blocks, barriers, and other "dead-weight." The only thought allowed to occupy and condition the winner's mind is that good, and only good, is and will continue to be one's constant expectation and experience. That means the winner forgets whatever happened that was not good in the past, sets new goals, and moves *forward* to achieve these goals—that is, the winner gets on with his/her life.

Condition your mind and it will change the condition of your life.

Forgiving, the Ultimate Freedom

Forgiving literally creates the *spiritual energy* that brings subsequent blessings directly to the forgiver. Think of what the word *forgiveness* means: "to give forth," or "to give in exchange." That means it is you, the offended one (supposed victim), who *first* give *something* to the person who offended or harmed you. That "something" might be the benefit of the doubt, a word of pardon, an expression of kindness, or even best wishes; or an acknowledgment that the matter is no longer a problem or conflicting issue, and that "bygones will be bygones."

By giving forth like this, your act of forgiveness creates the *exchange* of good-for-bad/healing-for-hurt/peace-for-pain that transforms your experience. To forgive is to set the prisoner free—and then discover the prisoner was you! Conscious, constant acts of forgiveness keep you in a continuous state of receiving blessings.

The Great Teacher Jesus admonishes us to forgive. As a matter of fact, his entire teaching was based on simply two things: Forgiveness and Love. Forgiving, as defined by the *American Heritage College Dictionary*, Third Edition, means "To excuse for a fault or an offense; to pardon." Forgiveness is an act of pardon by one who has been wronged or victimized by another.

Your forgiving the wrongdoer is less a "favor" you are doing him or her than a favor you are doing for *yourself*. You see, forgiving enables the "victim" to keep his/her mind free and spiritual lines open. Of course, the eternal and ultimate example of forgiveness is Jesus himself. The scriptures say that, while hanging on the cross, with his dying breath he petitioned God thus: "Father, forgive them [those who killed him] for they know not what they do." Similarly, the story of baseball greats, the late Los Angeles Dodgers catcher Johnny Roseboro and San Francsico Giants pitcher Juan Marichal, illuminates and clarifies the miracle-working power of forgiveness in the aftermath of a violent act.

Forgiveness is free; refusing to forgive can be very costly.

GOING FROM THE FIELD OF SHAME TO THE HALL OF FAME

In a tough and tense ball game between the Los Angeles Dodgers and the San Francisco Giants, Roseboro "buzzed" batter Marichal's head as he returned the ball to pitcher Sandy Koufax. An irritated Roseboro felt that Marichal, in previous innings, had thrown too many razor-sharp fastballs to a couple of Dodgers in an effort to "brush them back" from the plate or out of the batter's box completely.

Roseboro, crouching below Marichal, saw his chance to get even. The ball he hurled back to Koufax supposedly nicked Marichal's ear as it whizzed past his head. The baseball, launched by Roseboro's powerful arm, might as well have been a projectile.

Stunned and completely unprepared, Marichal slapped his open palm against his face and, upon finding that he somehow barely escaped serious injury, instantly turned around and began beating Roseboro over the head with his bat. Stunned fans and everybody on the baseball diamond looked on horrified as Marichal's assault raised a giant lump on Roseboro's head and caused a two-inch gash from which blood poured down his face. Both dugouts emptied onto the field as every Dodger and Giant within view came to his respective player's defense. The melee produced a seriously injured Johnny Roseboro and earned Juan Marichal a stiff fine and suspension; moreover, he narrowly avoided police arrest for assault and battery.

Many years after his retirement, Juan Marichal's name was repeatedly submitted to the board of directors of the Baseball Hall of Fame, in Cooperstown, New York. Each time, however, he was rejected for induction. Dismayed and disheartened, Marichal finally began to worry that his assault with his bat on Johnny Roseboro, almost twenty years prior, had come back to haunt him. He was seized with a sudden and unshakable fear that the ugly incident, regarded as one of baseball's most violent, would remain in the archives, if not in the minds of baseball's top brass, forever.

So from his home in the Dominican Republic Juan Marichal telephoned Johnny Roseboro in Los Angeles and asked him is he still held that incident against him. Roseboro said no. Then Marichal suggested that they meet and appear regularly together to show that neither harbored ill feelings toward the other. Roseboro readily agreed and flew to the Dominican Republic to appear in Marichal's golf tournament and show baseball fans and executives everywhere that they were friends. Roseboro, intent on chasing away the pain of that day long ago, reportedly could see no reason why he should not forgive Marichal.

Soon after, when reconsidering Juan Marichal's nomination, the board of directors approved his being inducted into the Baseball Hall of Fame. Instantly, Marichal knew that he was the beneficiary of a huge act of forgiveness. He telephoned Johnny Roseboro and with deep gratitude excitedly told him the news of his induction. Marichal viewed Roseboro as a remarkable man whom he had long ago forgiven. His hope had been that Roseboro would one day forgive him. The power of that forgiveness echoed throughout the world of baseball as news of Marichal's induction into the Baseball Hall of Fame spread like wildfire.

Forgiveness is a spiritual principle that frees the forgiving victim from the "past" and rewards him/her with authority and control of their present, and, of course, future. In her book *The Dynamic Laws of Prosperity,* Catherine Ponder states that forgiveness is an act causing a "vacuum" that forces Nature to fill it with only good for you, the forgiver. Your understanding of the fact that Nature abhors a vacuum should inspire you to forgive everybody who has ever hurt you, betrayed or deceived you, or otherwise conflicted with you. Forgive all such persons instantly and silently affirm, "There is no ill will between you and me. Only good occurs between us. I now view you with respect and understanding, and I continue to bless you and the good I see in, and wish for, you."

Use this affirmation or compose your own similar and uplifting words. This particular tool in your act of forgiveness is so powerful that Ponder describes actual cases in which forgivers experienced physical healings and financial success by deliberately creating—with their act of forgiveness—the "vacuum" that Nature could fill only with good and abundant blessing for them. Forgiveness clears and cleans the slate, settles the account. Your "account" thus empty and unoccupied with grudges, resentments, and negative feelings about others (or yourself), Nature goes to work to fill the vacuum you have created.

As surely as there is a law of gravity, Nature must use this vacuum. Ponder advises that whenever you experience lack or limitation in anything, you should immediately go into quiet meditation for at least thirty minutes, making this a daily practice and specifically forgiving all who have wronged you, while affirming good for them, until you experience the success and abundance you desire. And the anticipated success and abundance will occur every time.

Equally important as the apostle Paul's directive to "pray without ceasing" is the necessity of forgiving without ceasing. In the midst of your daily interactions with others, constantly practice the act of forgiveness. See others as well as yourself in the best light, blessed with your best thoughts. Doing this will help to make your "Forgiveness List" shorter at those times in your meditations specifically devoted to forgiveness. As you engage regularly in the forgiveness process, forgive yourself as well. This act is as important as forgiving, and being forgiven by, others.

In her book *How to Stay UP: Letters from Edna Lister,* Lister explains that if there appears to be delay in one's experiencing the result (healing, financial success, harmonious relationships) one desires, it is because full faith in the act of forgiveness has not been invested by the forgiver. The forgiveness process must be done diligently and with total and continuous faith; you cannot waver between hot and cold, or, worse, be lukewarm. Incomplete faith will result in *complete* failure.

The truth of your being is that you can never be hurt or harmed. Therefore, since there are never victims, only "volunteers" (throughout the tides of history, every so-called victim had a hand in his/her "victimization"), forgiveness is one of the two most important acts—the other being loving—that humans can and *must* perform to cleanse the mind and free the soul. Indeed, the best way to get even is to forgive...and forget it! Forgiveness, then, is itself an act of love performed at the highest spiritual level.

Forgiveness is the laser-sharp tool the winner uses to cut the ship's dead-weight anchor so that he/she can navigate on the high seas of success.

WHAT YOU CHOOSE IS HOW YOU WIN OR LOSE

In his powerful and practical book *Don't Sweat the Small Stuff...It's All Small Stuff,* Richard Carlson teaches that life is a matter of choosing what we allow to occupy our attention and our emotional space. In other words, it is we who can elect to weight ourselves down with the trials and tribulations of the world or to free our minds of them through the process of forgiveness and love. We can choose to get bogged in the swamp of our life's "soap operas," or we can choose to exert cause over them by using them as "teachable moments" and for learning and growing. Thus, we can make the choice to *soar* instead of *sink*.

There was once a prospector in the old wild West who went up in the mountains with his donkey in search of gold. He discovered a tremendous vein and immediately began to dig. His efforts were rewarded instantly. He placed every huge chunk of gold he found in the donkey's saddlebags. Finally, the saddlebags were overflowing. Overjoyed, he began his descent down the mountain to cash in on his tremendous find. Despite the incredible value of the gold on the donkey's back, the donkey's "thought" was of the sheer torture he was experiencing from the awfully heavy load on his back! We have more in common with that donkey than we care to admit!

> *There is gold in your life. It awaits your discovery now. Better to weight yourself down with gold's bullion than with life's burdens.*

SEE THE END AND SEIZE IT

A winner sees the end first. A winner keeps his/her eyes and attention on the prize. That is, a winner realizes that obstacles are seen only when one takes one's eyes *off* the goal. That's the only time obstacles appear. They simply do not exist when the mind and eye are filled with the goal.

Occasionally, race horses have blinders placed over their eyes. This is done because these particular horses are easily distracted by the activities and the environment around them, such as the movement of other horses or the actions of people on the sidelines. When they don't have the blinders on, it is difficult to get these horses in the starting gate—their eyes are literally filled with the distracting world around them.

With the blinders in place, however, their peripheral vision is blocked; the distractions cease to exist, and the horses can be led easily to the starting gate. At that point, all they see ahead of them is the finish line. This all-important goal completely fills up their vision. Now the *end* is firmly, fully, and *first* in sight. Getting there could only be accomplished by placing it as the first and only thing in the horse's sight.

A winner has the ability to see the end (goal) first and foremost and to understand the necessity of completing anything he undertakes and bringing it to fruition. Non-winners simply begin many projects and leave them unfinished. Thomas Edison had bulldog persistence when developing the light bulb. Despite encountering some 3,000 separate filament failures, he refused to accept these as *personal* failings on his part.

When asked why he never gave up and decided that the light bulb was an unrealistic dream, he happily explained that each time a filament failed, it gave him "one more opportunity to eliminate a defect." Many people would have stopped the process long before 3,000 defects doomed 3,000 filaments. They would

have resigned themselves to living in near darkness—
something many do anyway, modern technology
notwithstanding.

A winner has trials and tribulations like everyone
else but does not announce them to the world. One of
the basic qualities of a winner is the ability to walk
through life with a quiet mind, calm assurance, and
total peace. A winner rises up, goes through, and
endures. Although faced with challenges, a winner does
what is necessary to create a quiet mind and mentally
walks through the challenges. A winner deliberately
becomes conscious that the Holy Spirit is moving on
his/her behalf to correct the situation. Rather than
become frightened, embittered, or defeated by problems, a winner perceives challenges as opportunities to
learn and grow.

I once took my son and two of his cousins to an
amusement park. We climbed into those cars that go
through the haunted house—a three-minute ride.
Inside the house was a skeleton that made surprise "vis-
its" by popping up out of the floor. When that happened, all three of the boys would yell and scream in
fear. Of course I, as an adult, knew that these appearances were harmless and just mere show. So my mind
was not disturbed in the least. I was peaceful and content, because I knew it was an illusion. All challenges
are illusions. They are not the reality. The only reality is
God—the ANSWER to every problem.

A winner lives in the *solution* of the problem, not in
the problem itself. A winner knows that inherent in
every problem is its solution, no matter how obscure.
Therefore a winner directs his/her attention to finding
the solution and does not get bogged down by, or in,

the apparent problem. Thus, a winner's "light" (enlightenment) and understanding are not dimmed. A winner realizes that what is called a problem is really an *appearance*—merely a shadow, shape, or form without substance or structure. The Great Teacher Jesus warned that we should never judge by appearances. Therefore a winner does not *empower, energize,* or *stimulate* the problem by magnifying its powerless "shadow."

A winner is not hypnotized by the world of events, effects, and results, and therefore is not controlled by them. Baseball Hall of Fame great Hank Aaron struck out over 3,000 times before setting the then world record of 715 career home runs. Despite the fact that his strikeouts outnumbered his home runs, his mind was dominated by one thing only: *home runs.* He filled the "field" of his mind with thoughts of home runs and did not focus on his strikeouts; in fact, he ignored them. As Edison did with his failed filaments, Hank Aaron considered his strikeouts as mere "defects" that only propelled him closer to the experience of hitting home run after home run after home run.

Live in the energy of the solution, and the problem will die from lack of "care."

THE ART OF PERFECT VISION

If we gave more attention to the weeds in the garden than to the flowers, the flowers would be in trouble! Life works best when we focus on its gifts—love, joy, peace, kindness—rather than on hate, avarice, envy, revenge. When people who are married come to me and discuss the challenges in their relationship, I tell them that what they have forgotten, since they first met, is that the spotlight and energy was originally on presenting themselves in the best light, and always having their best foot forward—being the best they could be for each other. For example, they had a round of candlelight dinners, a bevy of floral sprays, a passion for hideaway trips, endless surprise events, and so forth. Then, after a couple of years passed, they seemed to have gotten "accustomed" to each other. In effect, they became like two old shoes around the house.

Their attention, or spotlight, was then deflected onto what *disturbed* them about one another. "Why do you leave toothpaste in the sink?" "Why do you always take the last piece of dessert?" "Why do you take so long getting ready whenever we have somewhere to go?" The truth is, they were doing those "irritating" things all along. The difference was that, in their blissful, new-romance and best-foot-forward period, their focus was on only the good they gave to and received from each other.

When I bring this to their attention, I also encourage them to go back in their minds to the beginning of their relationship and, to the extent possible, relive those wonderful, pleasant, and perfect experiences, letting themselves be overcome with the thoughts and feelings of those times. In that way, they revitalize and re-invigorate their love for each other and see each other in the same "best light" that embraced and nurtured them when they first met.

A successful marriage, or any successful relationship, is not only the result of finding the right person, it is the result of being the right person.

BACKWARD VISION IS BAD VISION

Our vision must be "consciously current." We cannot afford to look back and dwell on the past. We must stay in the "now," for, as we've already seen, it is all the time we have. The Bible tells the story of Lot's wife, who kept looking back and was turned into a pillar of salt.

What a powerful lesson *that* literally petrifying event teaches: anybody who looks to the past with trepidation, sorrow, anger, fear, and the like, becomes immobile in their thinking, rigid in their behavior, and lacks the drive and energy to move forward in a progressive, positive manner. Like Lot's wife, they can become petrified in their tracks.

When an automobile engine is turned on, energy is unleashed as a result of turning the key. If we put the gear in Reverse, the car will go backward. If we put it in Drive, the car will go forward. It is the same energy that propels the car in either direction. However, we are the ones who *choose* the gear.

It is infinitely more difficult to back down the freeway, turnpike, or expressway than it is to drive forward. The same principle applies to thinking. *Thought is energy.* We can choose to think back into the past—going in reverse with regret—or choose to move forward in peace and confidence. Make peace with the past. We cannot look through the rear-view mirror and expect to drive forward.

Sorrow looks back, worry looks around, but faith looks up.

BE LIKE A FLOWER—UNFOLD YOUR POWERS

While on a walk one morning, I approached a bird on the sidewalk, and as I got closer, it flew away. Its flight sparked a thought in my mind. How does a bird know how to fly? I reminded myself that birds were *born* knowing; no one had to teach them. It is something they do instinctively. Then I began to think about all life forms. How do they do whatever they do that is unique to their particular forms? For example, a fish instinctively knows how to be a fish; no one has to teach it.

There is an Intelligence in the Universe that resides in all things and that instinctively teaches life forms what to do and how to do it. The caterpillar—not just one or two or some, but *all* caterpillars—cannot resist building a cocoon around itself and transforming into a butterfly. A seed, when planted in the soil, bursts forth from within; there's an Intelligence within the seed that causes the seed to express itself in its likeness: as a tree, flower, plant, fruit, or vegetable. A rose seed must, from within itself, become a rose bush, an acorn must become a giant oak, an apple seed must produce an apple tree.

Let us now focus on us, as human beings. This Intelligence is in us at its highest level, and yet we are unhappy, afraid, sick, confused, filled with hate, anger, and frustration. Why? Because we don't allow this Intelligence to express in its fullness from within us. Unlike other life forms, we have to *learn* how to live, think, and be. Others who may be well-meaning but yet don't understand the true essence of life themselves—our parents, grandparents, uncles and aunts, teachers, friends, the government, society—nevertheless shape and mold our attitudes.

So instead of living from the inside out, as other life forms do—allowing this Intelligence to express fully from within themselves—we live from the outside in. And as a consequence, our creative and spiritual energies are weakened and blocked; the currents that flow simply stall and stop, like stagnant water. Often it is less a matter of us living our lives and more a matter of who and how many others we allow to *influence* our lives and make us sad and unhappy.

We were created to control our own destiny, including our attitudes and emotions. Being emotional slaves to others creates a master-servant relationship that is neither joyful nor justified. We must be free of emotional bondage in order to have the *capability* of expressing ourselves from the inside, and living from within, to create the kind of life we want on the "outside."

Your emotions have the power of lightning. Take charge of them, discover your own "electricity," and light up your world.

BEGGING AND PLEADING AIN'T PRAYING

If you pray on your knees or with your head bowed, put an end to that practice immediately. You're just wrinkling and messing up your dress or canceling the crease in your pants; and there is no god down there in those regions where your head is bowed. Lift your head, and affirm with certainty that God is right where you are, right now, desiring and willing to give you the kingdom.

The kingdom is any good thing that you are capable of imagining yourself having, without harming another. There is no god that is reluctant to give to us, nor is there one who withholds anything from us. Our inability—and even refusal—to see life's larger picture, to see life in all of its glory and grandeur and magnificence and abundance, is what keeps us from experiencing our good.

The Great Teacher Jesus said, "All that the Father [the Source of your life] has is yours." The majority of people believe that seeing is believing. In other words, they refuse to believe something until they see it demonstrated or made "real" first. Dr. Wayne Dyer, motivational speaker and counselor, stresses in his book *You'll See It When You Believe It* that we need to unlearn what we have been conditioned to believe.

Said another way: we have been going south when we should have been going north. It is our *belief*, first, that brings into being what we desire. Our belief determines when and if we will *ever* see what it is that we desire. Indeed, our belief enables us to see: to imagine it (our desire or goal), to know it and fully accept it, in mind. Reverse your thinking—the belief/"horse" must go before the see/"cart"—and train yourself to *believe* first and foremost; then that which you desire will come to you.

So when you pray, instead of begging and pleading to a god up "there" somewhere, let your prayer be one of affirmation, affirming—knowing and believing— that your good is already at hand, available to you *now*. There is no need to struggle, to shout, to whimper, moan and whine. Too many people offer up their prayers to God—with claw marks all over them!

Prayer is not an act of war; you need not take on the role of, nor consider yourself to be, a "prayer warrior."

You need only *affirm*; that is, *acknowledge* that your good (goal) is already made available to you; that your need is fulfilled; and that your problem is solved. Again, the Great Teacher Jesus, in the Book of Luke 17:20, 21, states that the kingdom of good is not "lo here nor lo there," nor does it come by observation, (that is, you cannot see it "out there" somewhere). He simply said, "The kingdom of heaven [or good] is within you."

So then, since my good is within me, the responsibility that I have to myself, in order to experience it, is to learn how to access and obtain it. And I do that by affirming with absolute certainty that the good that I desire is now mine. I live in *that* consciousness—knowingness—until what I want, desire, or need has become reality in my outer world. If I am diligent—if I work on myself conscientiously—the God that Jesus spoke of, which is forever within me, will always respond.

With a strong belief "muscle" and affirmative prayer, you will receive heaven's blessings as surely as day follows night: how you pray is how you get "paid."

LIFE: A SMOKY BATTLEFIELD?

When we pray, we must remind ourselves that we are not asking God to change Its mind; instead, we are really doing the work that is necessary to *change our belief* that God is reluctant to give to us. The act of affirmative prayer is a spiritual kind of "workout" that *conditions* us to believe and accept the good that God has already promised and provided for us.

One of the many prayers I vividly remember hearing as a child was "Lord, O Lord, come down here and help us on this old smoky battlefield called life." Though said in earnest, nonetheless this kind of prayer is flawed. It represents the "faith" of one who believes that God is far beyond, somewhere up and away in heaven's remote reaches and must climb down into the "smoky battlefield" of life.

This kind of prayer is a distortion of the beauty and wonder of life and shows the petitioner to be pessimistic and, possibly, depressed—a major sign of lack of faith. Such prayers only demonstrate a *firm* unbelief and rejection of all that God has already provided. While those who pray in this manner may argue that they believe in God, that is *not* the point. The point is, we must also believe that our good—in every sense of the word—as the Great Teacher Jesus told us, has been provided in advance for us by the very God to whom many *howl* their prayers.

Again, the Great Teacher Jesus said that all that the Father has is already yours. And simply that "It [the miracle/blessing/ answer/desired goal] is done unto you as *you* believe." Not as God believes nor as Jesus believes, but as *you* believe. It is you who must choose to activate and use your *power* of belief.

If you believe that God is far off in the sky somewhere and removed from human events, then that becomes your truth (experience). If you believe that life is a "smoky battlefield," then that weird and eerie concept also becomes your truth (experience). Not God's truth nor Jesus' truth, but *your* truth. *What you believe becomes your experience. Belief is what CREATES it!* Could the vast numbers and kinds of religions, as well as the vast quantities of houses of worship, all over the world, be a telltale sign that we have missed the point in a million different ways?

The reality is that the Great Teacher Jesus spoke and led by example, the best form of teaching. Yet, the manner in which we pray shows that (1) we don't believe, or (2) we don't understand, or (3) we were not paying attention. *Few of us pray anything like Jesus prayed!*

If you were to give someone the advice of your highly successful *example* and experience—in golf, tennis, losing weight, best car deals, investing, or anything else—and the person seeking the advice always ignored it and even did the *opposite* of what you advised, wouldn't you be a little concerned, maybe even insulted, especially if that person repeatedly sought your advice and ignored it? Well, have you ever thought of the possibility that we might be insulting God by the manner in which we pray?

The scriptures say that before Jesus did anything "he looked up and gave thanks," meaning that he lifted his consciousness to a higher place of acceptance and gave thanks that whatever his desire/need was at that time had already been fulfilled or achieved. And then he told each of us, "The things I've done you can do too." Constantly leading by example, Jesus was *proving* to us how to live life to its fullest, most joyful, most rewarding, and completely unlimited possibilities—exactly as God intended.

> *Pray in the knowledge that God operates your life through you as effortlessly as your car "lets" you drive it through the roads and across the expressways.*

THE BEGGAR PRINCE

We are *more* than God's children. *We are God in form.* Literally, we are DIVINE ROYALTY. Yet we often act like the beggar prince who, ignorant about his royal heritage and wealthy lineage, sat soiled and unkempt by the roadside and begged every day, trusting that strangers might at least look his way and give to him from the pity in their hearts. Rain or shine, there he was, slumped by the roadside, begging. One day, a very important-looking stranger stepped out of his coach, walked over to the beggar, and gave him a large wad of money. Instantly, the beggar's eyes lit up. "Why, thank you sir, thank you!" he repeated fervently.

His eyes glowed with the feverish gratitude of the desperate and forlorn, as he alternately stared at the money that over-filled his hand and gazed upon this kind and important-looking man. The man nodded curtly and started to turn around and walk back to his coach. Instantly, he stopped.

What is that glint of gold, somewhere near the beggar, that just struck my eye? he asked himself. He turned back around and looked at the beggar still sitting awestruck and transfixed by the treasure he held in his hand. The man walked over to the beggar very slowly, puzzled, carefully eyeing the garment he wore. It was filthy and wrinkled beyond belief. As he got closer to the beggar, he began to smell the stench in the air around him. *What was that gold glint I just saw?* He asked himself again.

Finally, a mere foot away from the beggar, the man bent forward and saw what had earlier, for the briefest moment, caught his eye with its brilliant flash. Hidden beneath the dirt caked on the beggar's garment was an intricate and elaborate stitching of the purest gold. When the sunlight struck it just right, the gold radiated; but when the man moved his head ever so slightly, its gleam was gone, as if a cloud had blanketed it.

The man had to work to find the gold again. He turned his head this way and that way; he shifted his body to the left and then to the right; and he even stepped a few paces away to be sure he was not bringing shadow into the sunlight. There it was again! The gold gleamed, seemingly brighter than before. The man gasped and clutched his heart

Thinking nothing of the filthy garment, nor having any regard for his own impeccable suit of clothes, he began to brush the dirt from half of one sleeve of the garment and, to his surprise, saw that the hue of its cloth was deep purple; the gown was cut from a priceless, imported silk. *Why, this looks like a royal garment!* The thought racked his brain over and over. Unable to contain himself, he threw off his coat and began brushing the rest of the sleeve furiously.

He examined the freshly cleaned material accented with brilliant gold stitching. The weave was deep and stood out in bold, gold relief. He stared at the rest of the filthy garment. *Could it be that the rest of the garment was made like this?* he timidly asked himself. His entire body quivering in nervous anticipation and excitement, his two hands suddenly became a blur as he went to work with lightning speed and brushed, scrubbed, and scraped all the dirt off the entire garment—pounding and peeling, clapping and clawing; and sweeping the dust and beating the dirt away—until, hours later, the sun had sunk deep in the western sky.

Breathless, he stepped back to appraise the result, and almost fainted where he stood. There, in front of him, before his very own eyes, sat the beggar in a garment that gleamed like new! Gone were the filth, the stench, and the wrinkles. And what a sight it was to behold. The deep purple silk was completely embroidered throughout with the finest gold. Each silken pocket sparkled with a golden royal crest and coat-of-arms. The purple-and-gold glare was so radiant, the stunned man had to bring his trembling hand up to shade his eyes.

Nearly speechless and choking from the dust of his labors, he turned to the beggar—who still sat shocked and delighted, counting and re-counting the fortune in his hand. "Uh, er…your Royal Highness, please forgive me," the man began. "I-I-I, uh, failed to recognize you," he stammered; I don't know why. I b-b-beseech you and beg your eternal forgiveness." His head remained bowed as he said this.

The beggar looked up toward the voice that had just spoken and saw a man who was truly embarrassed, perhaps even frightened. As he raised his arm, the beggar suddenly caught a glimpse of his own gleaming sleeve and gasped. Not believing what he saw, he looked again and squinted and shielded his eyes from the radiance of his garment. He scrambled to his feet and the wad of money dropped from his hand. Ignoring it, he rose to his full stature; the important-looking man before him now knew that, just as he suspected, he was in the company of true royalty.

The beggar ran both hands down the front of his garment and shook his head in disbelief. He rubbed his eyes and opened and shut them time and again. His eyes and hands told him the texture was the finest; the gold, the purest. Then he ran his fingers through the hair on his head; finally, he rubbed both palms roughly over his face and tugged at his beard. It was clear that he was self-conscious and wanted to look presentable. But it was the words he spoke that struck at the very heart and went to the soul of the man who stood watching him humbly and with the deepest respect.

"Sir, it is *you* to whom *I* owe a debt of eternal gratitude! Thank you for showing me who I *really* am. I am a Prince in the Royal Court of the King. Though I once had dominion throughout the kingdom, I lost dominion over myself. Come with me. I shall make you Chancellor of Education. I once was blind but now I see, thanks to what you taught me—by *showing* me. I therefore want you to teach my royal subjects throughout the kingdom."

The two men climbed aboard the coach. In the fading yet still-bright light of the late afternoon the coach suddenly turned a deep purple color, and every door was instantly emblazoned with the royal crest and coat of arms in gold. The horses turned and headed instinctively onto the road to the Court of the King and cantered smartly beneath their purple blankets with woven stitching of the purest of gold.

Dust off your royal garment, rise to your feet and rule life from within your royal court.

GOD: NEARER THAN THE LIGHT OF DAY

The scriptures tell us that God is nearer than our hands and feet, nearer than our neck vein. That all-intelligent energy which is God is the spirit, the life force, the mind, the love, the joy, the power, the presence that is within you and within me. Therefore when you pray, it isn't necessary that you scream, shout, and argue with yourself, for you are the expression of that which God is. Actually, we should "walk" through life as silently as we can. Our prayers should be quiet and gentle, reassuring ourselves constantly that God is for us; and we should always be consciously aware of living on the affirmative side of life.

There is a beautiful compound called the Self-Realization Center, on Sunset Boulevard and Pacific Coast Highway, in Southern California. At this site the great Hindu teacher Paramahansa Yogananda built a beautiful, man-made lake with a little worship chapel for 75-100 people to congregate, and a trail that winds around the perimeter of the lake. There are seats all around, flowers, plants, and trees where you can sit and meditate. The diameter is about a half mile. The lake is inhabited by a few geese and ducks. A small bookstore sells metaphysical and New Thought reading materials. A small cottage houses a cadre of monks.

As soon as you drive onto the grounds, you immediately realize it would be impossibly inappropriate to yell or scream. That recognition alone speaks volumes. This wonderful place itself seems to suggest that visitors be silent while contemplating the presence of God, which is within us. It has been said that our only two natural fears are those of loud noises and great heights. So you certainly do not want to frighten God by yelling and screaming at Him. Promise yourself never to do that.

Calmly know that life is wide awake and waits patiently for you to rouse yourself from your "sleep" and take possession of the gifts that are your Divine birthright.

TIME: IT HAPPENS ONLY NOW

Jesus prayed in the present time—all of his verbs were in the present tense—and so must we. In reality, the only time there ever is, is this very moment—*whenever* "this" moment is. We can never go back into the past, even for a second, nor can we go into the future. We can only experience "the moment," which is perhaps the most difficult thing a person can do, because our minds are so undisciplined.

In any given moment most people are either reviewing some distasteful experience that occurred in the past—regretting it, wishing they had "it" to do all over again—or fearing some event that is to take place at some time in the future. They all but abandon the joy, the good, the peace, the love that should be experienced in the moment.

We live our lives much like the person who, after having lived by a railroad track for an extended period of time, gets accustomed to the noise of the trains going by, and simply does not consciously hear them anymore. Similarly, the "noise" of the world dulls our awareness of the abundant and limitless good that is to be experienced by living in the "now."

I am reminded of a scene in a great little movie, *The Gods, They Must Be Crazy*. Two secretaries who worked at a large city newspaper talked incessantly. One day, during a break, they were sitting in the courtyard, doing what they usually did—talk, engaged in a nonstop conversation. Suddenly they paused, having nothing to say for about 30 seconds. Finally, one turned to the other and asked, "Is the noise in my head disturbing you?"

In much the same way, we live out of synch and out of touch with the God within us. So alienated are we from Its eternal, internal power and presence, that we grow uncomfortable in the "quiet of the Infinite." Needing noise, much like the addict needing his "fix," we beckon for the blast of life that is *outside* ourselves. And it is in the nerve-jarring, bone-jangling carousel of *that* circus that our lives, instead of being distinguished, become distorted.

If you look at the globe, it looks divided—by different oceans, lakes, seas. The appearance is that earth itself is divided. The reality is that if you were able to drain the water off the earth, you would see that there is *one* body of land. There is likewise one life, one body, one mind. All that we are using, we are using by the grace of God. What we create, we create out of our consciousness by inspiration from God.

We have been given dominion over all things on this earth plane, so let's constantly remind ourselves to take dominion over our lives—the thoughts that we think and the feelings that flow from those thoughts.

> *You need only one tool in life—your calm belief. And it works in the same way all your life: to create in your outer domain the real expression of those things that lie in the dominion of your thought.*

YOUR "GREEN APPLE" AFFIRMATION #4

Affirmations are mental and verbal *confirmations* of your total and complete belief in your desires, plans, and goals. We enthusiastically encourage you to say your affirmations repeatedly, daily, *and* meditate on them. It will do you so much good to *hear* your affirmations in your own voice. Meditating on them is like wearing a comfortable, warm, and favorite coat: the feeling is so right.

Meditation is spiritual *medication*. It is your Rx for success and can be powerful and instantly effective. The more you meditate on affirmations and say them, the more you SEE them take form and shape in your life. They are your God-given power to create your world as you wish it to be. Do not underestimate their solid, consistent, and reliable universal power. Remember: *FIRM* is a key part of the word *Affirmation*.

And never forget: *it was with the SPOKEN WORD—affirmation—that God created the heavens and the earth.*

Say and see the following Green Apple Affirmation:

Today I desire only to discover more of who and what I am. I affirm my power to choose happiness and well-being for myself and my fellow-man. I fill my mind with thoughts of peace, poise, power and confidence, and these become my reality. I declare, with certainty, that my good and I are one. I take the time to laugh and to play. I am a joy to all who know me. I live in the light of truth and wisdom. I declare, with authority, "Let there be Light," and there is light. I release all conditions that are no longer of service to me. Grateful for the lessons learned, I welcome new good in my life. I open Life's door, the good within me calls, and I follow for these gifts of awareness. I give thanks.

CHAPTER 5

PRAY LIKE YOU BREATHE...WITHOUT CEASING

IT IS OUR FIRM BELIEF that in the scriptural passage where Jesus directs us to "pray without ceasing," biblical translators omit from this three-word directive the idea or connotation that we are to pray *affirmatively*. What Jesus *meant* is just as important as what he may literally have said. And scholars are none too sure about that either—their published opinions outnumber the various versions of the Bible.

Praying correctly is no less important than eating correctly, walking correctly, or breathing correctly. Somehow biblical scholars, while underscoring the need to pray, overlooked the *how* of it all—that is, the *way* to pray according to Jesus' directions and God's pleasure. Without this vital key to prayer that a correct interpretation of Jesus' command would have afforded us, we humans have been locked in mass confusion, complete uncertainty, and largely unfruitful prayers and have reaped unfulfilled lives for thousands of years.

It is painfully obvious that the human dance on the floor of history has been bound, not in the arms of peace, happiness, and abundance, but in the embrace of war, disease, poverty, global pollution, and famine. Our seemingly endless disasters through the march of time simply prove that we have not only failed to pray (properly), but, as a result, *we have prayed to fail!*

Because of that crucial omission by biblical translators about how, exactly, to pray, we do not *include* this additional dimension as part of Jesus' directive. This exclusion causes us to miss the full significance of his command. You see, in reality, we are *always* praying—with every thought we think. Every thought is a prayer; and we think without ceasing. That is how we are created, and there is nothing we can do to change this very human characteristic.

What Jesus actually meant by his directive is that we are to be ever mindful—vigilant—about the *kinds* of thoughts we think, making certain they are affirmative, purposeful, and uplifting. Why? Because ALL prayers are *answered!* No prayer goes ignored. In other words, everything humankind has ever prayed for, it has received. Likewise, every experience—good or bad—that humankind has ever faced, has been brought about by, and is the result of, its prayers (thoughts).

Our thoughts are the fastest and most powerful prayers we humans will ever have. They are our instant, constant, and most potent tools for change.

YOU GET WHAT YOU PRAY FOR

We may not like what we have received—that is, the fruits of our prayers—or we may "explain" them away by saying that our wishes were never answered. But the plain truth is that all prayers get answered. If we open our eyes and see the circumstances and events that surround us—whether in our personal lives or in the outer society—*they are the direct result of our prayers.*

Ignorance and misunderstanding of how to pray do not exempt you from experiencing the condition or circumstance that you bring about by your thinking (praying). In other words, your accidental ignorance does not grant you immunity from the results. That is why you must understand *how* to pray correctly. It is of urgent importance that you understand you can change your life by changing how you pray.

Knowing how to pray—and treating prayer like the art and science that it is—ensures that your life experiences will change and turn out exactly as you wish them to be. Rather than complain about "unanswered prayers," you will be able to sing about the "prayer miracles" that seem to flood into your life the moment you think and/or speak your prayers. Since we created our human history by how (*badly!*) we prayed, we can also create a different future—by changing our present prayers!

As a quick look at history will prove, we have been praying negatively because we have been *thinking* negatively—and vice versa. Our human experiences become negative as a result of our train of thought. Jesus was saying, be mindful—consciously aware—of the thoughts that you, as an individual, think. Too many people put more time and attention on choosing their dinner menu than on selecting the right "menu" of thoughts they let enter their minds. Determine now to take the first step to make sure your thoughts are filled with the desires of the heart—bouquets not bombs, compliments not curses, plenty not poverty, and love not loathing.

As Confucius, the great Chinese philosopher said, "The journey of a thousand miles begins with the first step." We believe that he was telling all humankind that the journey to their good is in consciousness by their being aware, moment to moment and step by step, of that to which they give their attention and plant, cultivate, and grow in the "garden" of their mind—as thought.

The majority of live radio talk shows have what is called a "seven-second delay." This delay gives talk-show producers an opportunity to delete inappropriate callers' utterances, such as profanity or obscenity, before they go out onto the airwaves. The seven-second delay makes radio programming much easier because it allows producers to screen and delete most prohibited verbiage before they become a reality to the listening audience.

Thoughts are things. So screen them—and you'll get the best that life brings.

LISTENING, THE KEY TO WHAT'S MISSING

Likewise, as our own "radio producers," we should *listen* to the thoughts we are thinking before we utter them. Imposing our own "seven-second delay" is a good exercise to practice constantly, because it corresponds to what Confucius and Jesus had in mind—imposing a seven-second delay before beginning one's 1,000-mile journey, using the delay to block all negative thinking and affording the opportunity to practice and perfect affirmative prayer. Begin now the mental journey of supervising and controlling (screening) your thoughts. You are both host and producer of your own "thought show."

Do every single thing in prayer. Keep your antenna (attention) high and constantly rising up to God and to God alone. To be fully grounded in and directed by God, you simply cannot allow your attention to wander aimlessly. Like a magnet, it can easily attract and pick up the wrong things. Your attention is a powerful form of mental energy that works for you only when you control and direct it. You cannot put your attention on negative thoughts and expect positive results. And you cannot let your mind be home to *both* positive and negative thinking.

The study of Physics proves that two opposing forces cannot occupy the same space at the same kind. One must stay, the other must leave. We cannot be wet and dry, hot and cold at the same time. We cannot go up or down, turn left and right, experience light and darkness at the same time. In like manner, we cannot think of God *and* something other than God. We cannot be full of faith and, at the same time, be full of fear. What we are is the result of the *kind* of thinking that we allow to dominate our mind.

Tune the "radio" of your mind—let God's thoughts be your only station.

TUNING LIFE'S MOST IMPORTANT INSTRUMENT: YOURSELF

We must always remind ourselves that when we pray, we are not seeking to change God's mind, but to change *our* mind—to put our thinking in harmony with that which is God-like. Let's view this in terms of how musicians prepare for performances.

I have done concerts with symphony orchestras. Just before we would rehearse, the conductor would ask the pianist to play an "A" on the piano. One hundred and twenty-five other musicians onstage, with various instruments, would instantly tune their instruments to the piano, considered the "source" instrument.

All the brass, woodwind, and string instruments would be tuned and re-tuned repeatedly until every instrument played the perfect "A"—in harmony with the "A" from the piano. Everybody knew the standard of tonality was the piano, the "source" instrument. Equally important, they also had to be in tune with each other.

As individuals, we are much like musical instruments—the violins, the trumpets, the violas, the drums, the pianos, and the flutes. God, in a manner of speaking, is the piano, the Source. We must hear, understand, and accept God's "tone" in order to tune our minds to it, through prayer. Only constant, conscious attentiveness and alignment to the Presence (God) within will enable us to play the "melodies" of our lives in the key of God's harmony.

God's nature is love, peace, beauty, truth, joy, perfection, wholeness. Therefore we must acknowledge and achieve God's harmony in order to "tune" our thinking (praying). The individual musical instrument, no matter who is playing it, *must* be in tune with the source instrument; otherwise, the instruments are considered out of tune, something judged as unacceptable.

Several years ago in southern California, there was a weather oddity called "El Niño"—and "El Niño" happens in California to a lesser degree than it happens anywhere else. It is a peculiar atmospheric energy that makes for strange weather patterns. During the winter months, El Nino created a weather front that was very windy, cloudy, and rainy. Dark clouds filled the sky almost every day. Most people focused primarily on the "strangeness" of the clouds and the rain and the stormy conditions.

However, the truth that would have made the difference, had we known this truth, was that if we wanted to experience the sun, that could have been accomplished by going out to Los Angeles International Airport, purchasing a ticket, to, say, Phoenix, and within five minutes after takeoff, we would have been sitting on top of the clouds and experiencing the sun all around us. The sun is always shining, regardless of the appearance of clouds, storms, winds, hail, or any other atmospheric energies that "conceal" the truth. The truth is what is real; nothing else is. That is what we must keep uppermost in our hearts and minds.

Always remember: truth may seem to be in short supply, but its supply always exceeds the demand. The Great Teacher Jesus advised: "But seek ye first the kingdom of God...." It is your seeking this kingdom (truth) that enables you to SEE God's purpose and subsequently brings you rulership (control over your life) and limitless blessings that are yours by Divine birthright.

ANSWERS EXIST ONLY TO BE FOUND

In our daily living, we must realize, as Jesus did, that although we sometimes experience what seem to be tremendous challenges that create the appearance of stormy conditions in our lives, we must rise in consciousness to a place where we say, with absolute certainty, that life is good. Jesus always did this, for example, by concentrating his attention upon the solution rather than on the (appearance of the) problem. Since he was the example, or way-shower, then it is essential that we do as best we can to follow in his footsteps.

When Jesus told us that the "table is prepared before us" and that our "cups would run over," and "greater good than I do shall you do," he was declaring not only the absolute goodness and grandness of life itself but also life's *ever-increasing* goodness. If we are to experience the good and grand life, it is only possible to do so by taking Jesus completely at his word. To use a sports analogy, Jesus was our quarterback: he ran the ball, made the plays, wrote the playbook. He provided us—by his attitude, thought, and action—a permanent "gameplan" for success in all things. What a perfect "model" to have!

> *Oceanographers report that despite the mighty turbulence at sea, at a mere one-foot depth below the surface are waters that are calm and peaceful. The still and calm Presence of God within you is your guide through the waves of life that only seem to be crashing around you.*

WHO, WHAT, AND WHERE IS THE CHRIST?

Christ is a word that means the presence of God or Spirit in man. There have been a few individuals, throughout the march of time, who have demonstrated to an extremely high degree, the light and life of God in them. Jesus, Buddha, Gandhi, Dr. George Washington Carver, and Mother Teresa—to name a few—are some who have been so connected to their Source that they literally radiated with the light of God—the very Christ-consciousness—in all they set out to do. Their attitude, understanding, acceptance, and faith in God as the Source of everything empowered them beyond ordinary standards of success.

A simple analogy might serve to clarify this. Think of how a light dimmer-switch works. There are count-less levels or intensities of light that can be obtained simply by how we turn the dimmer-switch. This basic fact applies to our awareness of our relationship to God. The more we understand this relationship and consciously live it—through the expression and radi-ance of the Christ-light within us—the greater is the good that comes our way. Indeed, to others we might appear to be miracle-workers, such are the abundance and diversity of blessings we enjoy. Our life becomes illuminated like a once-darkened room bathed in inescapable light. We have succeeded in turning on our internal dimmer-switch to full power, to reveal the Christ-light.

Consciously connect to your Source and see the obvious results of living through your Christ-consciousness.

THE LORD'S PRAYER MUST BE OUR PRAYER

There are many words that have different meanings in different languages and cultures. For example, the word *father* in the Aramaic language that Jesus spoke is *abba* and has a totally different connotation from the word *father* as we use it. *Father*, in English, refers to a male being in a physical form. *Abba* means "loving presence" and "Divine intelligence."

So when Jesus uttered the Lord's Prayer, the greatest prayer ever spoken, he began it by saying, "Our Father"—yours and mine—because he knew that this infinite presence and love that God is, which permeates the Universe and created us, is the same loving presence that created him. In other words, what Jesus was seeking to share with us was the truth that we are all made out of the same substance, the same "stuff."

Therefore when we pray, we don't pray *to* it; we pray *as* it. Jesus said, "I and my father [this infinite love and wisdom] are one." He knew there was no place where *It* ended and *he* began. That is why he said, "our." He knew that the same principle applied to all mankind throughout eternity. We can never be separated from this loving presence.

There may always be a human *sense* of separation; but the reality is that we can never be separated. What accounts for that sometimes persistent sense of separation? It begins within us at the moment we start to believe in two powers: God *and* something else. There is only, and there has always only been, *one* power. And so our prayer should be one of affirmation—affirming our oneness—in order that we may heal, within ourselves, this false belief and sense of separation.

The Lord's Prayer is a spiritual mind treatment. That is its purpose. And each phrase has power because of that Divine purpose. The reason that it is uttered in the present tense is identical to the reason we breathe: to reveal life and the presence of the Spirit. That is, the Lord's Prayer is a living, dynamic, Spirit-filled oration. It is powerful, purposeful, and perfect in structure and tone, composed expressly for us by the Divine Presence that brought into existence the heavens and earth.

> Our Father, who are in heaven [*indicating that it is an entity/presence/energy*], hallowed be your name [*sacred is thy nature*]. Your kingdom is come [*your good is available to me right now*]; your will is done on earth [*in my human affairs*] as it is in heaven [*in my spiritual experience*]. You give us this day our daily bread [*the ideas that are necessary for the fulfillment of my good*] and you for-give us our debts [*you give us good in exchange for our missing the mark*] as we forgive our debtors [*it is done to us as we ourselves do*]. You lead us not into temptation [*you are only Good*], but you deliver us from evil [*by revealing its ultimate unreality*], for yours is the kingdom [*within me*], the power [*omnipotence*], and the glory [*illumination*], forever. Amen. [*And so it is.*]

For an example of what the Lord's Prayer becomes in the thought of one who makes full, personal identification with the Divine in her life and teaching, here is Malinda Elliott Cramer's spiritual rendering as given in her foundational New Thought textbook, *Divine Science & Healing*. Note that the first-person pronoun ("I") is to be adopted by the one praying the prayer:

FULFILLMENT OF THE LORD'S PRAYER

I, Father, am in Heaven,
Hallowed is my name.
My Kingdom is come,
My will is done,
In (creating) earth as it is in Heaven.
I give this day my daily bread,
And forgive debts as debtors are forgiven.
I lead not into temptation,
But deliver from all evil.
For mine is the Kingdom, and
The power, and the glory, for ever.
Amen. (p. 106)

When we have a physical ailment, we usually go to a medical doctor for a diagnosis, whereupon medication is frequently prescribed. The purpose of the medication is to eliminate the symptoms of the ailment and effect a cure. When a person says the Lord's Prayer properly and with deep feeling and conviction, it is a spiritual medication that will *treat* away the negativity that is in that person's consciousness. The Lord's Prayer, said properly, does the same thing in consciousness that the doctor's medication does in the patient's body: it makes the correction—in perfect, Divine, right order.

> *Stay "prayed up" by calmly working in the consciousness of God and seeing God in action, in everyone and everything you encounter.*

LIVING TO THE LIMIT OR LIMITING OUR LIVING

Do not put limits on yourself or your possessions. God does not know the difference between a goldfish and a whale, nor does God know whether you have much wealth or none at all. There is a wonderful old movie, *Lost Horizon*, in which there is a mythical city called Shangri-La. All of the inhabitants of Shangri-La are 300–400 years old, but they look like they are in their twenties. A visitor from the Western world one day asks the spiritual leader, Chang, how this could be. How could everyone look 20 years old but really be 300 or 400 years old?

Chang's immediate reply is, "We don't have birthdays. Because every time one has a birthday, he places another fence around his mind." What Chang meant was that the people of Shangri-La did not limit themselves by anchoring their lives to numbers signifying birth years and thus robbing themselves of life-energy. Said another way, they lived with full faith and belief in the goodness and infiniteness of life—and in their ability to increase life's unlimited goodness by consciously contributing to it. Instead of living walled in by birthdays, they demanded from life infinitely more than what a fixation on numerical ages would permit.

In their journey through life, most people do not realize that the mind is like a magnet attracting pieces of metal (*mental*) debris to it. Most of us handle problems in the same ineffective way—by drawing them to us and letting them cling and climb all over and around us. We simply invite them in, give them "space," snuggle up close to them; and, of course, they grow, overtake us, and then weight us down, becoming difficult to dis-lodge and remove (solve).

The result is that we wander through life feeling over-burdened, overcome, and undermined. Few real-ize that the same "problem-prone" power we *choose* to use, to bind ourselves to life's difficulties, oddities, and complexities, can be instantly used instead to find the solutions. We tend to become mired in the problem, but we ought to use our energy to *mine* (explore/dig for) the solution. Those who live in the solution simply do not have problems. They saturate their attitudes, thoughts, and feelings with confident expectation of solutions, driven by their unwavering faith and belief.

Every problem disappears when you find and implement its solution. And every problem has the seeds of its solution already sown in the problem itself. Make your thinking and lifestyle *solution-oriented* and problems will become strangers to you. To find any, you will have to search far and wide and hard and long for them—they simply won't stay around.

> *Soar to the solution, see the answer. Don't seize—or be seized by—the problem.*

THE ANSWERS ARE ALWAYS IN YOU

There was a man who had been in prison for over twenty years. One day he was lying on his bunk and an intuitive urging forced him to rise: he had a sudden feeling that the door to his cell would open—and it did. He walked down the hallway and past the security checkpoint only to find that the officers were busily engaged in conversation with each other and took absolutely no notice of him. He literally walked past them to freedom.

When confronting our own problems, trials, and tribulations we can likewise open the door to our mind—the truth of our being—to find that this is a limitless, loving Universe. And since we are one with this Universe, in reality we are limitless beings who, by *mining our mind*, can bask in the sunlight of freedom and enjoy every kind of success. In reality, we mete out our own justice upon ourselves, whether that justice is for our good or not. Said another way, we are both the *producers* and *consumers* of our own experiences. And in our journey through life, we are our own jailers and liberators.

Often when something happens that is not to our liking, we immediately look outside ourselves to a nonentity—for example, to the "devil" or to some individual or system, or to anything else outside ourselves—and point to them, blaming them for our misfortune and discontent. But when we have an experience that we like or do something that produces a benefit for us, have you noticed that we usually say (or hint or imply), "See what I did?" The truth, however, is that we created *both* experiences—the one leading to misfortune and the one bringing us the good of which we boast.

The Universe is filled with abundant answers for your every need.

New Thought Is the Most Important Subject That We Can Study

The New Thought philosophy places the responsibility for one's life in one's own hands. New Thought adherents regard God as an eternally loving creator who, as stated in the Book of Genesis, decreed, "Let us make man in our image, after our likeness." This explicit and precise declaration candidly reveals the special and spiritual origins of our creation: by Divine decree we are made in the image of both our Creator God *and* the other heavenly beings (they are also mirror images of the Creator) present when God made this declaration.

You might think of this Divine utterance and the creative act that followed as being somewhat analogous to a statement by a cinematographer who, with his camera trained on himself, directs his assistants—all of whose individual cameras are wired into his instrument—to capture his image in their own lenses and simultaneously magnify it (either in single or multiple shots) on the blank wall in front of them all.

Just as that image would be displayed for viewing on their wall, we humans, as the image of God, are proudly and lovingly displayed and viewed by God in our various "poses" on the wall of life. Our journey in life is enlightened and enhanced when we recognize our Divine origin and consciously accept that our human role on earth is to fulfill God's heavenly intent and purpose. It bears restating that we were born, and remain, as spiritual beings embarked on a human journey.

Our New Thought spiritual evolvement and enlightenment come about, in part, by our constant realization of our divinity and recognition of our oneness—our "image and likeness"—with God. New Thought can enable us to rid ourselves of: man-made religious myths and deceptions; wholesale mis-translations of scriptures demeaning our value to God ("conceived in sin and shaped in iniquity" and all our righteousnesses are "as filthy rags"); and a mythical, degraded, demeaning depiction of God as calling forth a "judgment day" ablaze with an eternal hell.

As God's spiritual intent is expressed through us, God would never destroy us. We humans are infinitely too loved by and too valuable to God to be destroyed; moreover, the *indestructible spirit* of God resides in us. God's wanting to judge and destroy much of the human race, yet (according to "old thought" religion) confer "salvation" upon a fortunate few, is a "bum rap" with which religious leaders and their followers have libeled and slandered God for millennia. It is simply not true.

God is not an avenging deity, angered by and depressed about the "human condition." The truth is, we are our own enslavers and saviors. We must be consciously attuned to and guided by the Divine Presence residing within every one of us. Our deliberate decision to thus connect with God is our sole means for changing and correcting our human conditions, freeing ourselves, and literally bringing heaven upon earth.

We occupy a Universe of absolute, unchangeable, immutable law; and at the same time, this Universe is filled with love. It is essential that we come to a place where we begin to recognize and realize that Universal Law governs our lives constantly. *For example, when is the law of gravity not being gravity?*

Our greatest responsibility to ourselves is not the job that we go to during the course of the day nor anything else with which we concern ourselves in the world of events, results, and effects. Our greatest responsibility is to understand the universal laws that govern our lives. To the same extent that we understand and apply these laws, we reap pain or pleasure, success or failure.

We are *physical-world-oriented*. We look outward and believe and insist that what we experience with our eyes, ears, and senses of taste and smell makes up, leads to, or proves The Reality. And we make life judgments that are based on, or biased by, our five physical senses. This false belief creates the appearance of life being a constant gamble—sometimes good, sometimes bad.

There's an old song, composed and sung by African-American slaves, titled, "Nobody Knows the Trouble I've Seen." Part of the words of this song are: "Sometimes I'm up, sometimes I'm down." But the truth is that life simply is—it is a complete and never-ending state of *is-ness*—only that which is good, perfect, and whole. This is eternally true despite the horrifying human-inspired incidents of slavery, slaughter, oppression, and devastation—events imprinted, as it were, with blood on the pages of history as a stark warning of what can happen when we abandon our spirituality and alienate ourselves from our Creator God.

Our responsibility to ourselves and to one another, as we have seen, is to recognize this truth. Such recognition brings about new thinking and a new way of living. Remember: Jesus said, "You cannot pour new wine into old bottles." You must remove antiquated, negative ideas from the "old bottle" of your mind and fill it with the "new wine" of fresh, new ideas. When you do this, old, undesirable problems will float away, and you will begin to encounter new and desirable experiences. These new experiences will be your reassurance that it is only *new* ideas that solve old, persistent problems— no matter how old or persistent!

The great jazz trumpeter Miles Davis refused, after a number of years, to play his old music. He believed with all his heart that only the newness of invention and innovation afforded him strength and vision to define and redefine his art. His artistic explorations were as much a triumph of the new as they were a put-down of the old.

Feel the Divine energy within, see life with God's eyes, set your goals and seize your dreams.

NEW THOUGHT WORKS WHEN YOU WORK IT

I have a very dear friend, Dr. Johnnie Colemon, senior minister of the Christ Universal Temple, in Chicago, whose favorite statement is, "It works when you work it," meaning life works for you when you work with it. She is adamant in her teaching regarding prosperity because she believes, as do I, that all humanity lives in an abundant and limitless Universe, which gives and gives and gives—and it will remain that way forever and always.

Our fears, which we pile up like pieces of unburned wood by the fireplace, prevent us from experiencing the infinite good that is ever available in the Universe. There is no person, power, or force that can stop us from experiencing our good except ourselves. As stated elsewhere in this book, if we believe that we can be, do, or have something, we are right. If we believe we can't be, do, or have something, we are *also* right. That is the reason the Master Teacher Jesus said, "It is done unto you *as you believe.*" Your experience is the direct result of your belief (thinking).

Life in its truest and purest form is much like a potter's clay. A potter takes the clay and shapes and forms it into anything that he or she chooses: cup, saucer, vase, platter, plate, bowl. The same principle applies to life. We are the potter; life is the clay. We are forever forming and shaping life into experiences and events that are exact replicas of the kinds of thoughts we think.

When Mahatma Gandhi was on this earth plane, his one desire was to free the people of India from their physical and mental bondage. When they became completely frustrated and began to riot in the streets, Gandhi would immediately begin to fast. He knew that he was revered and that his fasting would take the people's attention away from rioting and place it on himself and his welfare. Once, after having fasted for over three months, he was very weak and was visited by a reporter on assignment in India. The reporter asked Gandhi how he felt. Gandhi is reputed to have replied, "HUNGRY!!"

This story illustrates an important point. We must *hunger* for the truth; only then will it "feed" us. We must desire to know and become fully aware of the truth that God's gifts of abundant love, peace, joy, and beauty, as well as material things, are always for and available to us. Again, it is only the quality and newness of our thinking—constantly renewed with truth—that fills us and makes life consistently "new" for us.

You deserve the best, so expect the best. God loves you infinitely and has already prepared your good for you. Love yourself enough to claim it.

CAPSIZING IN YOUR OWN STORMY SEAS

You must have the "keep-from-drowning" instinct to break free of your limiting ideas. Many years ago, when great ocean-going ships traveled the seas, they would encounter tremendous storms that tossed them about—the cargo, the passengers—and as a result of this, the gyrostabilizer was invented. Because of its balancing and stabilizing force, it is an instrument that, since its invention, has found a home in all the world's ocean-liners. The result is that these gigantic ships now ply the great waters of the earth, regardless of the conditions of those waters, in relative peace and calm.

Deep within each of us lies a spiritual "gyrostabilizer"—God—and when we give It our conscious attention and activate It in our daily living, It will guide us safely and peacefully and calmly through the fierce storms and choppy high seas of life. The responsibility to activate this power, this presence, this instrument, always rests with us. Nobody else can do it for us.

My good friend the comedian Redd Foxx told a story about his being a lifeguard instructor. He said that on the last day of the six-week training course, he asked his students if there was anything that had not been covered during the course.

One of the students said, "Yes; I'd like to know: if I'm on the beach one evening at dusk, alone, and I hear a voice out in the ocean calling for help, and I swim out to this voice and the person is in serious trouble, about to go do down for the proverbial third time, and for whatever reason they look at me and don't want me to rescue them—in that circumstance, what should I do?" Redd's reply to the student was, "Cup your hand like a miniature megaphone, place it over your mouth, look the person directly in the eye, and very emphatically tell them: 'Goodby.'"

In the process of living, because of the different levels of consciousness that people occupy, it is often nearly impossible to say the words or do the things that would be their saving grace. More often than not, it is necessary that we simply "live" the spiritual life and afford others the opportunity to see us as a wholesome and positive example. If they are ready, they will use us as their role model and change the thinking that will change their life. We cannot force somebody's "salvation" upon them. That is the reason Jesus said, "When you see me, you've seen the Father"—in other words, LIFE in action. And then he also said, "Follow me," meaning: "If you choose to, live life as I live it."

Life holds you "response-able"—able to respond— and <u>corresponds</u> accordingly.

YOUR "GREEN APPLE" AFFIRMATION #5

Affirmations are mental and verbal *confirmations* of your total and complete belief in your desires, plans, and goals. We enthusiastically encourage you to say your affirmations repeatedly, daily, *and* meditate on them. It will do you so much good to *hear* your affirmations in your own voice. Meditating on them is like wearing a comfortable, warm, and favorite coat: the feeling is so right.

Meditation is spiritual *medication*. It is your Rx for success and can be powerful and instantly effective. The more you meditate on affirmations and say them, the more you SEE them take form and shape in your life. They are your God-given power to create your world as you wish it to be. Do not underestimate their solid, consistent, and reliable universal power. Remember: *FIRM* is a key part of the word *Affirmation*.

And never forget: *it was with the SPOKEN WORD—affirmation—that God created the heavens and the earth.*

Say and see the following Green Apple:

I speak my word knowing that it does not return to me void. I speak the experiences of my life into expression because the power of creation is in my word and in my thinking. I consciously release Divine Power through my word because I know there is a Power greater than I am, and It resides in me. I know that this Power guides and protects me and is always aware of my every move. As I draw closer and closer to my beloved God Self, more and more I participate in Miracles. Thank you, God, for the greatest miracle of all—my life—the beginningless and endless part of me, the eternal reality of me, the everlasting Power within me. Thou art my whole being. And so it is.

CHAPTER 6

CHOICES, NOT CONDITIONS, MAKE AND CHANGE YOUR LIFE

MY FATHER lived in Leesville, a small town in Louisiana. He was the only person in his family to go to college. His father had been a farmer; that was the only life he knew. After beginning college, my father would return home every year during summer vacation. My grandfather would always meet him at the train station and take him directly to the farm where, almost immediately, my father began plowing acre after acre, field upon field. This continued every day during the long, hot summer until it was time to return to school in the fall. Understandably, fall was my father's favorite time of the year!

It never seemed to occur to my grandfather to inquire of my father how school was going or whether he liked it. My grandfather just did not demonstrate any sort of interest in my father's education. And it certainly never occurred to him to allow my father to take a break from farming, even for a day or two, and do something else instead. All my grandfather knew was farming, and he saw in my father the exact image of himself—another farmer.

Years later, in reflecting on his upbringing, my father confided to me that he hated farming. Although he was expert at it (how could he *not* be), he desperately did not want to be a farmer or have anything to do with the farming life. His heart and mind were not in it, and his greatest fear was that he would end up being a farmer. In fact, he said he feared the future if it meant farming.

He noticed that every summer day, at the same time of day, a freight train would pass near a remote corner of the huge farm. He would always watch as it moved very slowly. It seemed to be going only at the rate of one or two miles per hour, as if patiently waiting for him. And my dad would say to himself, "I wonder where that train is going." Somehow, the train represented the future to him.

He told me that on the last day of the summer after his senior year had ended, the train came through as usual. The listless movement of its wheels on the tracks and the noise of the boxcars jostling back and forth resonated in a steady cadence. As he stared transfixed, this rhythmic din on the open prairie became like a drumbeat seemingly summoning him insistently aboard.

The thought of being a "graduate farmer," who had completed his senior year in college, was as oppressive and intolerable as the mid-day heat. Suddenly, my father knew that he had to do something; so he climbed on his mule and headed it toward the freight train. The mule, sensing some urgency, ambled along at a faster-then-usual pace. When my father reached the train, he jumped off the mule and tied it to a tree nearby. Without looking back, he sprinted for the train and hopped aboard.

Savoring the memory of that incident, he looked at

me with a wistful smile and said, "Son, that was thirty-five years ago. And if nobody has gone down to untie that mule, he is still standing there, tied to that tree." You see, my father had a greater vision of life than that which was being presented to him in Leesville. Although farming was the only view of life that his father—my grandfather—had, farming was not in my father's vision at all. But getting a formal education *was* an important part of his vision. Spurred by his successful completion of college, he continued on and eventually earned a doctorate in sociology.

You are the captain of your ship, authorized to sail where your vision leads.

THE REALLY LOW LIFE

One of the greatest tragedies in life is that many of us stumble, stagger, or float through it, unaware or unconcerned. Blind to life's infinite possibilities, we short-change ourselves. We humans are the only life-form on this planet that has the capacity to live a life *less* than that which our Creator intended. We choose, more often than not, to live at a far lesser level than what God has in mind for us. We are the only species that does this.

Animal, vegetable, mineral, and atomic life-forms live and exhibit all their properties at their fullest potential for the entirety of their life cycles. They don't know any better. They don't know they can't do, be, or have whatever it is! Totally foreign to them is the thought (choice) of allowing or accepting the limitations of a *reduced* life.

Xeno, the Greek philosopher, said that our greatest responsibility to ourselves is to unlearn that which we have learned. This "unlearning" process begins the important journey toward unlocking and freeing the human potential. Each step that we take in this journey results in both our seeing and our liberating the brilliant facets of life as we have never known them before. The world seems to sparkle around us; and like a precious jewel, our potential appears to glow with an uncommon brilliance.

Life, then, starts to hold increasingly greater value for us. And as we experience more and more success, we move toward, rather than away from, life. We become enlightened by our consciousness of the truth that life is, and works, for us. This is the consciousness that sustains us through the various passages of life. It is the consciousness that we must elevate and keep, for it works constantly to free us from the shackles of *learned* ignorance and bondage.

There was once a farmer who purchased a large amount of land. For about three or four years he alternated planting different types of crops. However, the soil, mostly rocky and lacking the vital necessities, failed to support crop life. The farmer labored year after year with no yield except a growing pile of rocks for his efforts. Finally, disillusioned and disgusted, he sold his land for a pittance and left.

Several years later he was traveling through the same region where his farm had been and was amazed to see the abundant, brisk activity taking place throughout the area. People and machines were everywhere. The air itself seemed vibrant and charged with a certain energy, and the entire area hummed with industry and activity. Curious, the farmer ventured a closer look. What he saw, everywhere, took his breath away.

The "rocks" he thought were merely rocks were really diamonds. He nearly fainted when he was told that the farm he had sold was now known as the Kimberly Diamond Mines. His failure to achieve the abundance and the good life he worked so hard for was due to his limited vision. Feeling unsuccessful and unsatisfied, he had literally sold out. Had he looked beyond the external appearance of the mountain of rocks and broken one or two of them open, he would have instantly realized his brilliant and incredibly wealthy fortune.

Believe in all your goodness and worth, and you will never despair or fail.

RENEWING THE MIND . . . FOR LIFE

We are only now coming into the realization that there is no end to life's good that is divinely ordained for us to have—absolutely no end. God's love, God's peace, God's wisdom, and God's blessings are all freely and fully available to us. Even money itself is, in reality, God in action.

The apostle Paul said, "Awake, thou that sleepeth, and be ye transformed by the renewing of your mind." He was simply yet frankly saying, "Awaken to the truth of your being, that you are an heir to God's kingdom and a beneficiary of the entire legacy of good that befalls an heir. But you must renew your mind." In order to experience a life-change—to be transformed—you must undergo a mind-change.

As you observe life—yours and that of others—you will see that we tend to pay a greater price for living a life of mediocrity. It is actually easier to live by renewing your mind, and ascending to life's heights, than it is to live a stagnant life at lesser levels than the Creator God intended. As someone once said, "Genius is bestowed [by God] but mediocrity is self-inflicted."

What humankind needs to fully and constantly realize is that we give birth to our individual experiences by the thoughts that we think. Life "works" like a mathematical formula. Think little, experience little. Think big, experience big. It was his grand vision of life that saved Abraham Lincoln from collapsing in utter failure despite losing many important elections for several years; losing his fiancée; being demoted from captain to private in the army; losing his child; and experiencing bankruptcy. His dogged determination to keep on, and his refusal to quit, came as a result of his disciplined thinking and his rock-solid conviction that brighter days lay ahead.

Each moment of your life is a "blank page" upon which you can write your success story.

GOD'S BLUEPRINT

The God for whom you work is really the Greater Idea of yourself. The reality of life is that we do not have a life of our own. The life that we are living is God's life, being lived in, through, and as us. That's the reason it is important for us to remind ourselves constantly that the real joy in life does not come from human results but rather from the joy in doing God's work and being God's channel through which Its power and presence constantly flow.

Thus, we let the "chips" (negative appearances, obstacles) fall where they may. It must be our conscious realization that we are working for God because, indeed, God is working for us—by working through us to do for us what we cannot do for ourselves. It is God's blueprint that *imprints* our lives. The more we embrace and embody this idea, the easier and the more joyful life's journey becomes.

An example will serve to clarify this point. The engine of a locomotive pulling a freight train of boxcars one to two miles long exerts over 98 percent of its energy in the effort of getting up the necessary momentum to leave the railroad yard. However, after it has journeyed out into the countryside, only 2 percent of its energy is necessary to keep the cars rolling. Our own (hypothetical) 98 percent *mental* energy exertion occurs when we size up the dimensions of a problem and do the mental work necessary to address and resolve it. The 2 percent energy displacement—a remarkable reduction in effort and stress—occurs when we realize that God's power flows through us to move us around and through the various storms and winds of life.

Operating under God's "steam" rather than under our own strain is what enables us to turn problems into profits, stress into success, and barriers into banners of triumph. Thus life with God—*as* God—becomes a joyous life. We elevate our lives to whatever levels we desire only by lifting up and cherishing the idea of God living as us. It is that realization and its subsequent "miracles" which enable us to understand that everything we do is, and must be, for the glorification of God.

Military forces around the world, when they are at war, have a slogan that goes, "God is on our side." There is no such God who chooses opposing sides. God has no idea of wars that take place, because all wars that are fought on the battlefield have always been first fought in the minds of men. Peace and prosperity can come only by *our* moving and separating ourselves away from the *personal* wars that *we* create in our minds. We can achieve this by realizing that life is an upward spiral, always moving us toward the realization that the ultimate realities—"fruits of the spirit," as the Bible calls them—are peace, love, joy, patience, and eternal good.

So, if in the past we were battered about emotionally by the vexations and vicissitudes of life, we must give constant and conscious attention to our thought process, making certain that we are living in harmony with that which is real: a sense of inner tranquility and contentment, self-worth, self-appreciation, and abundant success. As a tiny acorn grows into a giant oak tree, we must, as individuals, grow out of our "tiny-ness" into a giant realization of our oneness with our Divine self, God Allmighty.

There is only one side in life: God's side. That One side fits all. Get on that side.

LIFE AS YOU LIKE IT

As noted before, Henry David Thoreau said that most individuals live their lives "in quiet desperation." However, by recognizing and practicing the truth—that God operates in us, as us—to ensure that we avail ourselves of all the goodness It desires for us—we stand apart from such individuals and become immune to the adversities and misfortunes that come upon them.

In other words, though we are in the world, we are not of *their* world. Eliminating a negative condition, then, can be accomplished by *choosing* not to participate in, or have, it. As Dr. Frederick Eikerenkoetter (better known as "Reverend Ike") says, "The way for you to eliminate poverty in your experience is to not [choose to] be poor." Said another way, wherever you are in life, with respect to your financial condition, is where you have *chosen* to be.

What Rev. Ike means is that, as a "candidate" in life's constant campaign, you have *voted* for yourself and your position and condition—you are right in the middle of whatever circumstances surround you. Whether good or bad, they are there because you brought them into your experience. It is vital that you understand this fundamental truth. It is equally vital that you understand there is no virtue in descending to another person's level or joining their "poverty club" and "misery mind-set," to keep *down* appearances and make it seem as though you really haven't changed, despite your obvious material successes.

You *have* changed, because you *must* change. Do not deny your destiny and do not let others decry it. Blossom right in their midst, to the glory and gratitude of God. A rose does not strip itself bare of its lovely petals in an attempt to "keep it real" with the unsightly crab grass and weeds that cluster around and deface its petals. Continue to worship and follow the God in you, and grow wise and rich in Its abundant grace. Soon, as a result, others will bless the God in themselves and grow likewise.

A bird with a broken wing cannot fly. It is necessary that the wing undergo a healing process in order that the bird may express and experience itself as it was created to do. In like manner, an individual who would transform his or her broken life and fly high with new "wings" must recognize that his or her strength lies in their ability to see or understand the truth of their being, with respect to their oneness with their Source, the creative force and principle in the Universe.

There have been many individuals throughout millennia who have sought in many ways to bring this truth to the forefront for all to see. The greatest and most compelling was the Master Teacher Jesus, who said, "Upon this rock I will build my church." In reality, what he was alluding to was that his consciousness was built on a firm foundation of a spiritual connection with the Cause of all life: the omnipotent, omniscient, omnipresent One: the church he referred to was his mind. The "Rock" was his Creator from whom he obtained his ability to be firm and able to discipline himself and "see" (understand) life as it truly is—a powerful, beautiful, magnificent experience. The following story will clarify this well.

Two brothers were discussing their respective businesses one day. One of them, Bob, owned an extraordinarily large poultry farm with hundreds and hundreds of acres of chickens. As Bob showed his vast acreage and great number of chickens to Arnold, his brother, Arnold noticed an eagle strolling among them. He asked Bob why the eagle was walking with the chickens. Bob replied that when the eagle's mother laid the egg, she abandoned it. A hen, seeing the egg, sat on it and hatched it. Consequently, all of its life the eagle viewed itself as a chicken.

In disbelief, Arnold took the eagle on top of the garage, held it over his head, and demanded that it fly. The eagle did nothing. In disgust, Arnold took the bird and placed it back among the chickens. That night, unable to get the eagle out of his mind, Arnold tossed and turned, awaking early the next morning. Immediately, he set out looking for the eagle. After finding it, Arnold took it to the edge of a small hill. He raised the eagle over his head and told it, "Fly. You were *born* to fly." The eagle did nothing. In absolute amazement, Arnold took it down and placed in back among the chickens.

The third morning, after spending another restless night, he found the eagle again and carried it to the top of a great mountain. He lifted it above his head and once again urged it to fly, to soar, to be all that it was born to be. Suddenly, the eagle let out a tremendous squawk and, for the first time in its life, spread its powerful, gigantic wings and flew. The chickens on that farm never saw the eagle again.

Think high, reach high, and life will send you soaring to its greatest heights.

LOOKING THROUGH THE GLASS DARKLY

Just as it was high time for that eagle to fly as it was meant to do, it is time that we cease thinking of ourselves as earthbound creatures and see the truth that the Great Teacher Jesus spoke of, the truth that sets us free, empowering us to stretch forth our wings and fly. We have always been wonderful, powerful, magnificent beings made in God's image and after God's likeness. As a matter of record, the scriptures state, "I have said that ye are gods and all of you are children of the Most High."

When we truly have this vision of ourselves, our lives will begin to soar. An eagle's strength lies not in its wings but in its vision. The same is true about us. Our real and enduring strength is not in our "wings"—the muscles in our arms, the sinews in our legs; our power is in how we use, and what we let occupy, our vision. Develop your vision, see the greater life, the perfect life, the whole life. See yourself centrally and totally connected with all of it. And watch yourself take off, guided by Divine power!

Several years ago, while on a self-empowerment retreat up in the San Bernardino Mountains, I introduced an exercise that would allow those in attendance to see for themselves how we have usually created false images of ourselves, and how necessary it is to correct those images. I brought two full-length mirrors: one that, like certain mirrors in amusement parks, distorts your image; the second, a standard mirror that reflects the image of one's body correctly.

There were about 50 people in attendance. I asked them to get in line and slowly, one by one, stand first in front of the false mirror, in order that they could see their bodies as they were *not*. I explained to them that as long as they stood in front of that particular mirror, that false image would be reflected back to them. However, any time they chose to see themselves as they truly were, all they had to do was simply stand in front of the standard, nondistorting mirror. As long as they stood in front of it, they would see themselves as they truly were.

For us, life is much like that—a "dance" with mirrors. The distorted idea and image of worthlessness, magnification of problems, and self-doubts are, in reality, the *false* images of ourselves that we have created and allowed to *mirror* what we regard as the reality of our being. All the while, however, we are perfect and whole, in every way. The true picture of ourselves, mirrored back to us, can only develop in the clarity of our mind centered in the true essence of our being—our godliness.

Therefore in your daily affairs, constantly remind yourself that you have options: you can see yourself in any manner (mirror) that you choose. And the results— positive or negative—are also of your *choosing*. So see yourself as you wish to be. Then reach up, stretch forth, and rise to meet your vision. Get to know, and become comfortable with, your "new" self.

Imagine your vision occupying a huge picture frame. Then practice *growing* into this frame and filling it up. You have the power to enlarge and expand your picture frame. Do this regularly, and each time fill up your new frame. Keep your vision *full* and your mind directed toward it.

God sees you as a Divine idea created from Its light, life, mind, and love.

CHOICE: LIFE'S VOICE

You have the power to choose your experience just as you choose your meals from a restaurant menu. What you choose to believe creates the resulting experience. Your belief is the key to the "ignition" of your experience. And when the key is turned on, your experience—like an automobile or aircraft—roars into life. All your experiences are real-life creations of your thoughts. It is your conscious choice that determines the *kinds* of experiences you will have.

There is no such thing as "I had no choice." Despite the pressures and bleak—or no—options that appear to stare us in the face, we always have choices. Desperation need not overwhelm us. As stated in previous pages, life greets you as you greet life. Feelings of desperation only breed and bring to you desperate experiences. Like a custom-made suit, your experiences are made to order. It is you who do both the making and the ordering of them.

The Universe was built and established from an idea. Everything in God's creation is spawned from and supported by ideas. There is nothing created without an idea. Nothing in life exists without an idea. You yourself are a Divine idea in the mind of God—the result of the Divine creative power expressing Itself as you. Think about it: there is no other you but you. You are unique. Billions of sperm cells died in the quest to fertilize the egg that eventually sheltered you at conception and nurtured your growth. Your cell survived the journey and emerged successfully to become the only you in the entire universe. Deliberately and specially conceived and planned, you were brought into existence by the Creator. You were not an "accident of birth." Indeed, there are no accidents of birth.

God *needs* you and therefore created you to fulfill that need. God invested in you the power to create and expand, enhance and empower your life *at will*. It is your ideas that enable you to do these, just as God's ideas about the Universe and life within it brought them into being. You, then, are a creator constantly creating by the ideas you possess. Whether you create masterpieces, monstrosities, or misrepresentations, the power to do *any* of this is fully and completely yours—nobody else's. Therefore you meet representations of yourself wherever you go. That is why it is so *very* important to see the world as you see your true self: *how you see yourself is exactly how the world will appear to be to you.*

Because we are evolving in our spiritual development and fulfilling God's grand purpose for us, we are the only form of life to which God has given the exclusive power to change its circumstances. Think about that and contemplate how powerful and wonderful you truly are! If the great dinosaurs, mollusks, raptors, and mammoths that used to roam this earth could have changed their circumstances or adapted to them, they might still be here. But, despite their size, strength and former dominance, they became *extinct* because they lacked the power to choose to change...and then change.

Unlike those great prehistoric animals, we humans can create the thoughts that create the experiences that involve and surround us. We create those experiences by what we *choose* to think. The power of choice is our greatest human power. Choice is a product of thought and cannot be separated from it. If you want a different experience, *change* your thought/choice. Remember: you are *always* experiencing the idea of your view of yourself. Regardless of what that experience is, it is based on how you see yourself. So look at your present experience/situation and analyze it. *Is it exactly what you want it to be? Are you happy with it? Do you want to keep it or change it?*

> *Choice is our greatest power. We are always using it. What are you choosing?*

THE HEART OF THE MATTER

As we continue to evolve spiritually, we come into a greater awareness and understanding of *who* we are. Similar to the activity of swimming or breathing, the truth keeps coming to us as we keep coming into it. This is the "second coming" spoken of so very often by the Great Teacher Jesus. Contrary to the theocracy of many traditional religions, Jesus' announcement and promise of the second coming has nothing to do with his returning to earth to judge it with condemnation, by dispatching countless millions of humans to eternal damnation and awarding others eternal paradise.

Because it is laced with denunciations of humankind, that particular superstition, masquerading as spiritual doctrine, has done an incredible amount of spiritual and emotional damage to humans for millennia and has demoralized and discouraged many who believe it. Jesus is not returning to earth ever again. It is we who must *choose* to *return* to Jesus by living our lives according to his teachings and fulfilling them by doing his deeds. As we have already noted, Jesus promised that "Greater deeds than I do, you shall also do."

"Greater deeds" were predicted of us (and, indeed, promised to us) because God loves us so *very* much (infinitely, eternally, and universally) and *chose* Jesus as our model for living. No greater story could ever be told. If life were a movie, Jesus would remain its greatest character, its ultimate star, its universal hero, its eternal example. *Why, then, do we cling obsessively to a belief of somehow being unfit and unworthy, suitable only to be judged, damned, and condemned (by God) to destruction?*

The scriptures state how powerful our choices are by admonishing us to: "Keep thy heart with all diligence, for out of it [your emotions/attitudes/thoughts] come the issues of life." Your heart is the storehouse of your thoughts, feelings, and emotions. You must *guard* your heart with your life. Let nothing reside in it that does not belong. What you hold in your heart is more important that what you hold in your hand. That is why Jesus said, concerning the telling of truth, "Out of the abundance of the heart, the mouth speaks."

Expressions such as the "heart of the matter," "she doesn't have her heart in it," and "take heart" illustrate the belief about the heart being a kind of vault for truth, desire, character, strength, and courage. Regardless of what takes place in the outer realm, we must remain unshakable in our faith. It is what is in the "inner realm" of our heart that makes, shapes, and changes our experience. How you choose to contact life—positively or negatively, or happily or unhappily—is how life will "contact" you and bring you (mirror back to you) the exact emotions you offer it.

Fear knocked on the door. Faith rose up to open it and found nothing there.

135

WHAT IS EXPECTED IS EXPRESSED

Expectation is an elevated thought, infused with desire, and is yours for the *choosing*. Choose to live with the *constant* expectation of good; that is the only way you will get it. Think of your journey in life as traveling on the "Expectation Expressway." What you choose to think and expect going, is what you will *meet* coming...back in your direction. Albert Einstein said, "You walk in the atmosphere of your beliefs." So upgrade your thinking—from "coach" to "first class." Better atmosphere!

Your mind is the most fertile "soil" in the entire universe. It *always* produces what you plant in it. Interestingly, as humans in love with our bodies, we spend considerable effort and attention to develop these bodies; yet we spend precious little effort to develop our minds. Learn to *love* your mind. It is eternal. The body is only temporary. Therefore spend your time and attention on developing—as the Apostle Paul stressed—the "mind of Christ Jesus": the Christ Consciousness within us. It is that development of the *mind* (not the body) that reveals to us our divinity. In truth, we don't *become* Divine; we already are. But as prospectors had to *find* the gold, first, we also have to *find* our divinity. The destination to our divinity is our most important journey (purpose) in life.

One of the most useful "choice tools" you have is your ability to filter out of your life that which is negative. Simply stated, don't give negative thoughts the time of day, not for even a mere second. Regularly filter them out. Just as you bathe your body, it is important to "bathe" your mind. Prohibit entry to thoughts that are not wholesome, healthy, good, enriching, enjoyable, kind, and loving. Keep your mind cleansed by filling it with only good thoughts of joy, peace, love, abundance, and positive expectations.

Don't spend much time holding or harboring negative thoughts, for "analytical" or other reasons. Release and let go of everything that is not working. Much like breathing in fresh air to overcome and neutralize stale air in the lungs, ingesting good thoughts constantly, and contemplating all of life's good, is the way to happiness and true spiritual and mental health. Choose to practice the Presence of God wherever you are—it matters not where!

Walt Whitman said, "Live as a conqueror and the world of limitations cannot infect you." That means to live as you *see* yourself. As we observed earlier, the mirror of your life is the picture you have placed there. So choose to see yourself as a winner (conqueror) no matter what the "odds" are, and the world (appearances) of limitations cannot block you. For when you see yourself as you truly are, and are meant to be, the entire Universe works on your behalf to enable you to realize that vision. The Universe is in tune with your thoughts and feelings. What are you putting "out there"?

The Universe is pregnant with ideas. We human beings are the avenue of birth for those ideas.

Faith Makes Your Fate

Whose life are you living? Are you doing what you want to do, being what you want to be? When all is said and done, what is the account of your life that is going to be written? Will the record show that you clung to problems, obsessed about "world conditions," felt trapped by poverty; or will the record show that you triumphantly overcame circumstances, ran through or hurdled over world conditions, and pushed poverty aside with wealth? Genesis tells us, "In the beginning God...." It does *not* say, "In the beginning, problems"! God is...ALWAYS. That is the consciousness you must have to surmount any challenge and live full and free in the grandness of life. As Wally Amos, the creator of Famous Amos Chocolate Chip Cookies, says in his book *The Cookie Never Crumbles: Inspirational Recipes for Everyday Living*: "God is the only Cook in the kitchen of your life."

Regularly ask yourself, "Where is my faith pointing me today?" Faith is your compass on the high seas of life. Know where you are going by knowing where your faith is. Locate your faith, and you locate your destination. Just as the atmosphere is full of air, you must operate on full faith. Such faith will lead you to know that life is never what it seems—it's always more! Each day of your life say: "This is the day the Lord has made. I will rejoice and be glad in it."

If this is the day the Lord has made, get your bloated nothingness—your attitude, misgivings, pride, doubts, resentment, hurt, arrogance—out of the way. This is your key to success and solving problems. Dr.

Frank Richelieu, Religious Science minister, shares this illustration of our willingness to impose limitations on ourselves, even after the evidence of previous, greater success: a flea has the ability to jump four to five feet high. If you put a flea in a mayonnaise jar, it will jump and hit the lid of the jar. Take off the lid, and what happens? The flea will still jump only up, lid-high. Now "programmed," it "thinks" it simply cannot jump out of the jar. So, it never does. Moral: don't think or be like the flea!

The Divine Presence resides in you. Its spirit in you lacks nothing. Spirit is the wholeness of God. God's Wholeness embraces us in a *healing unity* with our Creator. Our choosing to *unite* with God, and *untie* ourselves from our false beliefs, is the way to joy and happiness, health and healing, loving relationships, and abundant riches.

Dr. Richelieu also tells the story of Olympic snowboarder Chris Klug's experience as a recipient of a liver transplant. He won the Bronze medal in the 2002 Olympics, but 18 months prior to his Olympic achievement he needed a new liver. He received that liver and the doctors said he would need to take special drugs three times daily to avoid liver rejection. As Olympic champion Chris Klug stayed "up" on his medical regimen, per doctor's orders, we also ought to stay "prayed up" three times daily on our *spiritual* regimen.

Regardless of outward conditions, we can change our experience by choosing to change the condition of our mind. Just as God created the heavens and the earth to fill what the Bible describes as a void, we must use the creative power of God within us to create our world and lives just as we wish them to be. There is no better time to do that than right now, and there is no greater power with which to do it than the God-Power that resides in you and is instantly and constantly available to you.

There is an answer to every problem. Know it, believe it, desire it and live in it.

YOUR "GREEN APPLE" AFFIRMATION #6

Affirmations are mental and verbal *confirmations* of your total and complete belief in your desires, plans, and goals. We enthusiastically encourage you to say your affirmations repeatedly, daily, *and* meditate on them. It will do you so much good to *hear* your affirmations in your own voice. Meditating on them is like wearing a comfortable, warm, and favorite coat: the feeling is so right.

Meditation is spiritual *medication*. It is your Rx for success and can be powerful and instantly effective. The more you meditate on affirmations and say them, the more you SEE them take form and shape in your life. They are your God-given power to create your world as you wish it to be. Do not underestimate their solid, consistent, and reliable universal power. Remember: *FIRM* is a key part of the word *Affirmation.*

And never forget: *it was with the SPOKEN WORD—affirmation—that God created the heavens and the earth.*

Say and see the following Green Apple:

Good flows effortlessly through me. I accept the best that life has to offer. Today I take a fresh view of life. I am strengthened in my acceptance of the truth that I am one with God, now and forever. I like who and what I am, and I make a commitment to myself today to be good to me. I look for the right instead of the wrong in life. I give thanks for the increase of understanding that takes place in my life right now. My world is a miracle. I live in the joyous acceptance of this idea. And so it is.

CHAPTER 7

THE DAYS OF YOUR LIFE

ARE YOUR days spent in heaven, or are they spent in hell? The great actress and comedienne Mae West said that although she certainly had men in her life, she preferred life in her men. In light of this, you might ask yourself: "Do I have life in my days or am I merely counting the days of my life?" What things—issues, doubts, problems, regrets, and resentments—are you allowing to occupy your attention and absorb the days of your life? What kinds of *thoughts* do you let seize and control the life of your days?

Like boarders in search of a home, thoughts can easily "move in," set up housekeeping, and take up space. The longer they remain, the "fatter" and less mobile they get. But like the apartment-building manager who carefully screens would-be tenants, you must screen out negative and unproductive thoughts and let in the love, hope, joy, peace, wellness, and happiness to enliven your days.

God created the world, and all the life that inhabits it, declaring everything "good." You are an eternally important part of the goodness that God pronounced upon Its creation. Regardless of the outward appearance of things or conditions, the good that you wish—the *life* in your days—is already yours by Divine birthright. Your job—indeed, your life mission—is to acknowledge it, accept it, and act upon it. Goodness and badness are states of mind—the dwelling-place of heaven and hell.

Contrary to most traditional religious thought, hell is not a vast region or uninhabitable wasteland reserved for evildoers. And heaven is not some wondrous paradise where the "good people" are fitted with wings and spend an eternity drinking milk and honey and floating in the air. Hell and heaven are entities of the mind.

You are the thinker of the thoughts in the dominion of your mind. Your mind can become your prison or your paradise—the choice is yours to make. What do you choose?

THOUGHTS, THE FOUNDATION OF OUR EXPERIENCE

Abstract versus concrete, present and not future, heaven and hell are ideas that lead straight to, and verify, the current *instance*, or experience, that you can see in various forms almost everywhere you look. As abundant as is our thought, so too is the manifestation of that thought in our experience. How we think and what we think about determine *what* those thoughts grow into—what visible, physical *form* they take.

What we see—in our hearts and minds—is what we get. (Remember the great comedian Flip Wilson's constant declaration: *"What you see is what you get!"*) Indeed, it is humankind's collective thoughts that are transformed into their physical manifestations of the circumstances all around us: hell (war, famine, poverty, disease, and ruin), or heaven (beauty, abundant good, joy, peace, and well-being). Our experience is an expression of our thoughts. There can be no experience without the thought that brings that experience into being and sustains its life after it arrives.

"Collect your thoughts" is an expression that has been used as instruction for being calm, regaining focus, and maintaining control over nervousness and anxiety, as a prerequisite for handling a difficult situation. The confession "I was beside myself, I couldn't collect my thoughts" is understood to mean a lack of control over an intruding or unnerving circumstance and a strong sense of apartness from oneself.

One who controls the quality or content of one's thoughts through harrowing situations is said to have *presence of mind*. In truth, we all have presence of Mind—that eternal God-presence within us, which lives in and through us and activates us with Its energy. My great friend, the wonderfully talented actress and entertainer Della Reese, has a special saying that she utters constantly because it is so healing, uplifting, redeeming, and renewing. She even features this saying as the title of one of her books: *Strength Is the Energy of God*.

It is our conscious *awareness* of that Mind in us that makes the difference and gives us the control over situations we face—whatever and wherever they may be—so that we can experience the success we desire.

Think of your mind as having either the destructive power of a land mine or the wonderful and transforming power of a gold or platinum mine. Make your choice and take your pick. Decide to CHANGE your mind—focus it on the good you desire.

THE KEY TO LIFE

Consciously accepting the truth of our being and living in this truth are the missing ingredients necessary for putting back—as in *replacing*, since God made you whole, perfect, and complete—the *life* in your days. Otherwise, the emptiness of existence can reduce you to counting the days of your life: spending time in meaningless pursuits; confronting life with a "madditude" about everything; feeling cheated and of lessening worth; or seeing yourself as a victim rather than a *victor*.

We were created to do much more and much better than merely number our days. The key to life is discovering your true nature and its foundation. That "discovery" contains the power for going forward and conquering your fears and conceiving your dreams.

You can do all things once you fully realize your *oneness* with the Creator who made *all* things for you to do. Said another way, your days will take on a certain luster and brilliance once you realize that it is the God-light glowing in and through you that radiates in every part of your life. It is this understanding of your spiritual identity and connection with the Creator God that unifies you with Its wholeness and makes available to you the good that, through Its energy, will come to you at all times, in all ways, from all places, and in unlimited and unpredictable quantities.

Further, your recognition of your oneness with the Infinite makes the infinity of Its creation your treasure-filled storehouse of constant supply. When you unite with the Allness of God, your potential (which means "power") is unlocked. Unless you know and accept your true God-nature, you will be afflicted with a kind of spiritual identity crisis. As one person explained, "Until I realized who I *really* was, and that there was a Divine purpose for me, life felt like one long encounter with a fire-breathing dragon."

> *Our oneness with God is what makes life so "ONE-DERFUL." Every problem can be won by turning inward to the One who lives in us and does for us by working through us.*

SLAYING THE DRAGON

If you are constantly in the face of the fiery glow of life's "dragons," you have time for little else but to try to keep one leap ahead of the flame. No matter what you do to appease the dragon, it all seems hopeless. The dragon refuses to be pleased, and you fear your life is on the line. Your head throbs with the pain of your losing control of your own life. Your heart doesn't quite accept that your existence and the quality of your life are solely at the mercy or whim of others. Your power to influence—if you ever had it—no longer exists. And like a hunted prey, you feel closed in, tired and terrified. Your sense of self-worth has been diminished and your ego wounded. Paranoia—suspicion, fear, and mistrust—seems to accompany your every waking moment.

You see, when we perceive life as some kind of outside force—a chain—that weights us down, while the dragon spits fire and stalks, our perception becomes our prison. We feel isolated and alone; we may even wish to have some of that power we believe the dragon has. "*If you can't beat 'em, join 'em,*" might be the constant thought that seems like a practical proposition. The big mistake, though, is viewing *them*—life's various dragons, whoever and whatever they are—as having all the power and you having none.

Such a view of life is a common mistake and the reason why countless people feel *conquered* by life. Indeed, many find their existence is made up of daily battles in one long war. In such a struggle, you are psycho-emotionally and actively involved. You take things personally, regularly crying "foul." Reputation and prestige are cherished commodities that you won't compromise or have sacrificed. However, in order to win, you must realize that who you *think* you are is not who you *really* are.

In other words, you are not your *ego* and whatever other personality/self-identity/self-worth components upon which you have structured your "self." That is, your definition of who you are is just as flawed as trying to mail a letter without *defining* (providing) the address. Having no true destination, the letter ends up in the Postal Service's "dead letter" file or is returned to the sender.

> *The power to decide the kind of life you want is yours to use. You can have it if you want it.*

External God-Orientation (Ego)

Perhaps the biggest wild-goose chase of all is that in which we humans engage by seeking outside ourselves for ego gratification and social acceptance. So we play our social roles and wear our social masks; with practice, our "aliases" become complete. But the fear that we are never quite accepted (because we are somehow not quite good enough) keeps growing because what we really want, we realize we simply do not have: power.

We think that external approval from those in our social circle is the ultimate compliment. The constant puzzle, though, is why we always feel so empty. It is because we play our social roles according to rules *outside* ourselves, devised to serve *others'* needs, not ours. As their rules serve *them* and not us, so do we also serve *them* and not ourselves. A servant to another has abandoned his own destiny and greater life-purpose.

To be truly free and, of course, truly happy, you must realize that your True Self is—and has already been—completely free of the need to follow the roles and rules of somebody else. You must follow your True Self; if you don't, happiness will never be yours. You will only experience conflict, contradiction, and confusion. Why? Because your True Self is your spirit, your soul.

Your True Self has need of nothing: it knows that all that it "desires" already *is*. It has no need to struggle, to compare, to be jealous, to harbor anger or resentment, or to become cynical. In fact, your True Self does not even know what these behaviors and emotions are. Your True Self is immune to criticism and is fearless. It recognizes that everyone else is from the same Source, so it never feels superior or inferior to anybody. That is the difference between your ego self and your True Self.

Let go of, and separate yourself from, your ego and you will see how truly free you can be.

A Self Divided Cannot Stand . . . Itself!

Your ego—*External God-Oriented* self—can spend so much time away from your True Self that you can literally feel like you are capsizing and drowning in life's raging sea. Absent the conscious union with our True Self, it is little wonder that we have only our egos with which to navigate life. We then become like a ship that has veered dangerously off its course and its compass.

As Dr. Deepak Chopra observes in *The Seven Spiritual Laws of Success,* your True Self is your perfect compass. When you feel at odds with life, it is because you are not *at one with* your True Self. For example, lingering anger, anxiety, discomfort, and depression; feeling like a "square peg in a round hole" or a "fish out of water"; and an unshakable suspicion that life's cards are stacked against you are all just some of the warning signs that you are *apart from*—rather than *at one with*—your True Self.

One day a young man and his wife came to me and explained that they had fled their native country and had been literally running around the world trying to avoid the "curse" that was placed on the man by a powerful person back home. As soon as this curse was "put on" him, he and his wife immediately took flight. They explained that he knew his days were now numbered.

As proof, they showed me pictures taken when he was in his prime, in obviously robust health, playing soccer, cavorting with his children at home, reeling in a huge marlin on his fishing boat, and receiving community awards for various business development projects he created. I looked at these pictures and then looked at the man sitting before me. The difference was incredible and shocking. He was a mere shell of his former self. It was difficult to believe that the healthy, strapping, powerful, "driven" individual in the photos was the same underweight, highly distraught, jittery, and distracted man who sat before me and rambled, sometimes incoherently, his face dripping with perspiration.

The man and his wife pleaded with me for a "counter curse" to void or cancel out the curse supposedly placed on him by his countryman. I explained that only the man himself could void the curse. "As you sit before me, you can make up your mind right now that the curse, as you call it, no longer has any power over you and does not even exist. You can instantly regain the health and peace of mind you seek."

Both the man and his wife shook their heads vigorously. "You don't understand our culture," they explained. "When a curse is placed on you, you are doomed!" I tried to explain to them that the "doom" comes only by *accepting* the curse—by "taking it in." As I told them, denying the curse's power, and recognizing the Source of his True Power, would give this man complete and perfect protection from any and every kind of harm. Again, they shook their heads and continued to tell me, "You don't understand," and so forth and so on.

But it is *they* who did not understand. The man's ego and identity were so linked to the customs and traditions of his community that he *refused* to shake off the curse. He was persuaded that this was his lot in life and that he must spend his days desperately seeking a more powerful *human* force to ward off and void the curse. It was sad to look at this gaunt, haggard man, literally frightened out of his mind, yet totally *rejecting* the power he possessed to triumph over the curse that was destroying him.

You must understand that when you seek answers, not adversity; see solutions, not strife; and forgive your foes, not blame them: you are *working* with your True Self and *wielding* its power. Recognizing this power, and deliberately connecting with it, is to have *self-power*— directly linked to and fueled by your Source of True Power. And you can *feel* this power. With it, instead of driving your ship in somebody else's wind, you can hoist your own sails, set your compass, and find your own destiny.

The choice is yours. And your choice can *change* your entire life for the better. Unfortunately, this young man refused to believe that. He and his wife struggled to their feet, bade me goodbye, and left. I watched his bent form, slumped shoulders, and dejected expression. He was a lost ship, battered about by somebody else's ill winds—somebody who *wanted* to see him capsize in the bottomless, murky depths and crash against the deadly shoals. And this man was determined—through his outright rejection of his True Self and his True Power—to achieve that goal!

> *Your mind has the power to slay you, enslave you, or save you. Yet it operates only WITH your permission. It will do exactly as you tell it to do. What orders are you giving to it?*

How Others Control Your Destiny

As long as this unfortunate man continued to reach out and see himself connected to the evil power of the individual who had put the curse on him, he was driven by his *external god-orientation* (ego). If, on the other hand, he made the decision to *reach in* and *connect* with the God Power that was his True Self, in that very instant he would become whole and free. His refusing to recognize the falseness of ego—by denying or rejecting the curse—brought *true* effects of the curse upon him, no matter where in the world he sought refuge.

You see, ego-based power is not real, not true. Yet it lasts as long as your *attention* is on the thing to which *you* give this power. Ask yourself: *"What things do I give power to in my life?" "What are the curses that haunt me?" "Why do they have power over me?" "When will I make the decision to be whole and free?" "What is more important to me than making that decision right now?"*

The Great Teacher Jesus lived every second of his life with his attention on only what mattered most to him. Regardless of the view other people had of his work, he maintained full control over life. Life did not control him. Whether he was with Mary Magdalene, or feeding the multitudes with bread and fish, or changing water into wine for a magnificent wedding reception, he always placed his attention on that which he desired to control. Thus, he was *always* free. Being totally free, he was completely open and available to do the greater work of his father.

So dedicated was he to his spiritual mission, that he even chided his mother once with this reply: "I *must* be about my father's business." He understood the Source of his True Power; therefore, he understood himself. So permanent was his power, and so great was the effect he had on others, that his life, his name, and his works are etched in the human race's memory for all time.

The motor vehicle of life is yours to operate under your control. Whether you let somebody else "drive" your life, or whether you drive it yourself, is totally up to you.

JESUS, THE GREATEST EXAMPLE

Jesus' knowledge of himself and the corresponding self-power that followed literally drew people to him. Yet he promised humanity: "Greater things than I do, you shall also do." So confident was he of *our* ability to pattern our lives after his that he predicted greater accomplishments being done by those who understood his life and followed the light of his example. Unfortunately, the vast majority of humanity has misunderstood his teachings and condemns itself to living in darkness, blind to the light of his word and work.

It is impossible for you to fail if you have self-power rooted in the Source of all power. This power brings the right people to you for the right purposes and provides opportunities for you in random-seeming events. It is as though all nature marches to the beat of your drum and the sound of your trumpet. Indeed, that is precisely what happens. And there is a very good, a very logical and, most important, a very spiritual reason for this.

You see, Jesus was so powerful because he knew that he (the creation) and the Creator were one. And so it is with us. The same Creator who created Jesus is the same Creator who created us. We are one with the Creator. The Creator God expresses Itself—that is, Its identity—*through* us. We are God as humans, functioning as the body of God and enlivened with God's spirit. In brief, *we are God in action.*

When God decided to express Itself in human form, the result was, and is, *us.* God is happy—ecstatic, actually—to have Its home inside of us. But it is our grateful recognition and joyful acceptance of that which makes the difference between experiencing a hell of a life and life in heaven—since heaven and hell are right here, right now.

> *God gave you Its life AND the Great Teacher Jesus as your example. You are in the best partnership of all time...for all time!*

God's Greatest and Priceless Investment

God's "investment" (Its very presence) in you is the only power that is available to you for changing your life for the better. The power you place in the thoughts and ideas of others is only temporary and transparent power. Right inside you, giving life to every part of your being—your blood vessels, heart, lungs, capillaries, toes, fingers, eyes, etc.—is the same power that created the entire Universe.

As the scientist Dr. Neil DeGrasse Tyson stated on a PBS television program: "No longer can we view ourselves as separate from the universe; we are one with the universe. We are more than star-gazers. We were made with the exact elements that are in the stars themselves. We are star dust."

What a gigantic discovery that is! Don't you feel absolutely wonderful knowing that? Just think: you are fully supported by God and all of nature. God's investment in you and Its constant in-dwelling presence in you mean that everything happens *for* you—you can't lose in this thing called life, because life was made for you! So, start loving yourself; see the God in others and love them as a result; and start loving life in all its wonderful and infinite aspects.

Since life is both an invention and extension of God, it is only logical that we *depend* on God for *all* our needs. Depending on, or being influenced by, the circumstances—the quirks and oddities of life—is like following a mirage. We must, as the saying goes, "Let go and let God." By letting go of the weight of the past and the bonds of negative experiences, we become better at seeing who we really are, and, like an eagle, we can soar to the next level.

We must become so dependent on the God-power within us that we willingly let this Power replace the sum of all fears in our life. Instead of believing that "life-is-hard-and-then-you-die," we can and should live joyously and with the faith that moves mountains. Distractions, world events, conditions, and circumstances need not move us—because we are not, nor is our life, defined or decreed by them. That is not to say that negative events cannot or should not be changed. Indeed, they should—*by changing the thought that gave birth to them in the first place!*

> *God lives, and believes, in you. Therefore, believe in yourself and live your life IN God.*

THOUGHTS: LIFE'S MOST POWERFUL THINGS

Thought-power is creative power. It is the power that sparks action. Action, then, becomes directed behavior that produces an identifiable result. Good results come from good thoughts. Good thoughts are like a good foundation that is unshakable and permanent. Things do not appear without a thought having first given "life" to them. That is why it is so very important to understand that our true purpose, as spiritual beings, is to be anchored in the omnipotence and presence of God.

In this way our thoughts can be concentrated on the scriptural directive to "Seek first the kingdom of God and all its righteousness, and all these things shall be added unto you." That means to seek the *consciousness* of God. The *seeking* is the action that results in the *seeing* (finding) the kingdom—consciousness—of God right here. Entering the consciousness of God provides and enables us to seize the physical protection and spiritual nourishment we need. Remember this three-step discovery process for finding the kingdom of God: seek it, see it, and seize it.

The Great Teacher Jesus stood in the midst of the chaos in the world and said, "None of this moves me." He also said, "I am about my Father's business." As did Jesus, we must come into the "sovereign realization"— the royal domain—of the presence of God in our lives at all times. This realization should be our dominant thought, for it is *God's* dominant thought. God expresses Its life though us. And as Jesus did, we too will be able to see *through* world appearances by seeking and seeing (finding) God. The more we express God, then, the more we *experience* good.

> *Through your thoughts, you are creating all the time—even when you sleep. The "meals" of your experience are cooked in the kitchen of your mind. Change your "thought recipes" and watch your experiences change.*

TAPPING INTO THE GOD POWER

Knowing all of this is good. Most people who adhere to traditional religious beliefs not only do not know this, but they also would not believe it. So much in chains are we to either religious, philosophical, or even political dogmas, that we are seldom in tune with the Infinite. God's power is inherent in pure consciousness. To know this is fine, but to make use of it is far better.

How do you use this awesome and magnificent power, the very power that created the Universe and all the life that inhabits it? How can you tap into the creativity that flows, like a mighty river, through the consciousness of all life? Dr. Deepak Chopra suggests that a very good way is by exercising your mind through the daily practice of calm and expectant silence. This process, known as meditation, can be easily accomplished if you think of it as *listening* rather than *doing*. And this state of listening is best done by sitting quietly alone and relaxing by taking a few deep breaths. Rather than *willing* anything, simply *be;* that is, do not judge anything, try to solve problems, or go to sleep. Simply sit in a calm state of listening and expectation.

You might achieve better quiet concentration if you close your eyes.

Another good way to access the God-power that flows through all life is to spend time at the beach or in nature. Notice the quiet, towering hulk of a tree in the forest and every leaf on it receiving its full nourishment from it. While at the beach, hear the roar of the ocean, the lap of the waves, and gaze upon the sparkling sun-kissed sand. Be delighted in the harmony (cooperation and collaboration) of nature: how sea-gulls wait patiently for their food opportunities; how lovely, exotic "indoor" plants grow within the shade of powerful trees; how tiny beach birds use the ebb and flow of the tide as their "clock" for timing the finding of food. You will see that everything in nature occurs in perfect, Divine, right order—there are no accidents, only incidents. You will also see the infinite creativity, freedom, and peace in nature.

The sun "explodes" into earth's face in total silence. The sun contains infinitely more nuclear force and deadly gases than any quantity of "mass-destruction devices" human beings could ever bring into existence. Yet, the sun spreads its light and heat upon us without noisy and deafening announcement or fanfare and "parting shots." The sun simply *is*—and it shines always as it is.

You are God's light to the world; shine forth like the sun.

AWAKE AND MEDITATE

That is how we are to be—just as we truly are: without storm and stress. But that takes practice. So make a commitment to yourself to regularly practice sitting alone, say, when you first wake up in the morning, and simply be quiet with your eyes closed. In a state of complete relaxation, be at one with the Creator inside you. Hear only your breath and your heartbeat, not the last world-news report, family debate, or message left on your voice-mail.

Again, it is your quiet and expectant *listening* behavior that is the essence of your "silent treatment." With regular practice—morning, noon, and night—you will quickly achieve and assume power and solutions for every need. What you will experience are the effects of a *spiritual mind treatment*.

In order to obtain benefits from this miracle of silence, one has to make the same kind of commitment made when one decides to get up at the same time each morning and jog, swim, walk, or go to the gym for aerobics classes, weight-training, treadmill work, or whatever. The *constant regularity* of the physical and (in the case of meditation) *spiritual* commitment guarantees returns (benefits).

> *Develop a silence of mind and the "noise" of your life will vanish.*

Success: A Change of Habits

You may have to give up, cut back, or otherwise alter your current activities to make time for regular meditation. For example, if you are in the habit of reading the newspaper when you first get up in the morning, you may wish to discontinue doing that. Remember, your *perspective* on life is altered when you engage in regular meditation. Early-morning reading of newspapers tends to shape your perspective in the direction of the news. You may find your day unfolding in accordance with, and being "locked" in to, this perspective.

A more accurate term for newspaper might be "blues paper," since the information known as news is so very often bleak, depressing, and emotionally upsetting. Meditation, on the other hand, when done first thing in the morning, can attune you to the pure consciousness of the Infinite. Far better to thus allow the Infinite to "map out" your day than to "fall into" the puddles of printer's ink forming the graffiti we call newspaper headlines and front-page stories. Be willing to change whatever you need to change—habits and customs—to spend time in silent meditation, free of the interruptions caused by radio, television, bill-paying, and other "routine stuff." You will be happy with the results, for they are real.

> *Do not resist change; insist on it. Then watch your problems give way before the new opportunities that will present themselves to you.*

THE ABUNDANT GOOD LIFE . . . YOURS FOR THE TAKING

Every good in life you could ever imagine or will ever want—in all its variety and unlimited abundance—has already been ordained and created for you by the Infinite. Our eternal good *already* and always exists. All the Infinite requires is that we have faith and the vision to *see* our never-ending good. Regular and consistent meditation is the fastest and most efficient means for developing this vision.

Meditation is not *willing* your good to come to you. Rather, it is developing the quiet, reliant confidence of *knowing* that it is already there. Your attitude, desire, and goal are to be at-one with the Infinite and gratefully acknowledge that. Through meditation, the Infinite embraces you with the "Creator-consciousness." Without this, it is impossible to go deep within yourself to the faith, feeling, and fulfillment level where the Source communicates with the soul, resulting in your meeting both the supplier and supply of all your good.

In addition to practicing silence in the morning, take opportunities throughout the day to periodically practice being *silent*. At first, it may be difficult; you may continue to hear the "radio" between your ears rattling on about the staff meeting at work, the need to run some errands at lunch, the importance of returning a V.I.P.'s telephone call. But keep at it. In a very short time (a couple of days, perhaps) you will soon be very comfortable with the new and developing silence invading your mind.

You can produce your life exactly as you want it to be.

Minding Your Mind

You see, the mind understands that you have made the decision *not* to speak or even *think* thoughts that you would have spoken if you had not instead made the decision that "this is silence time." You are coming into your True Self, your pure spirit, and seeking to confront and address and access the Creator's power. Your *inten-*

tion to do this is recognized by the mind. It will cease its relentless thoughts about "urgent matters" and let you be in peace. The peace and silence you experience is the vacant and uncrowded region of pure power.

How long should you meditate? You should practice until you can comfortably meditate for at least 30 minutes—morning and evening—before stopping. The region of silent and pure power will confer a special awareness upon you. You will find your intuition, or "hunches" and premonitions, becoming sharper and more frequent and insistent. You will also become aware of the activity of cause and effect in your life; and as you see seemingly random events or people come into your experience and behave in an intelligible manner, you will realize that the Infinite constantly makes order out of chaos.

> *There are no accidents, only incidents. And "coincidences" are merely two events that were meant to occur at the same time.*

In Perfect, Divine, Right Order

Every event and every person crossing your experiential plane is part and product of the Infinite's power of correlating and organizing. As you realize what is occurring (that miracle phone-call "out of the blue," that long-due money owed you, that long-awaited contract, that indication that your special relationship with another is a "winner"), you will see that the parts, though "randomly" acting, are related to each other and related to the whole picture of your unfolding good. In this region of pure power everything is connected to everything else.

When discussing how meditation produces the clear inner vision so necessary to making life all that it is supposed to be, someone once said, "By going inside [through meditation] you gain insight." That is exactly what occurs.

> *Meditation grants you the inner vision that illuminates the answers to whatever ills may be in your life and provides you with the corrections for the conditions you want changed.*

FINDING GOD

For millennia humankind has pondered, debated, burned people at the stake, and waged wars over the question *Where is God?* We have become our own "loyal opposition" as we have refused to recognize the truth of our being and, therefore, the true presence (location) of God. One way to clearly understand *where* God is, is by analyzing a part of speech known as the "preposition." Words such as *in, of, with, by, for, through,* and *as* are called prepositions. We normally regard them as being the little words that, like a little salt, "season" a sentence as they clarify contextual (relational) meaning. Yet prepositions, when understood correctly, provide a powerful view about the relationship of God to us.

As we did before, let us again use part of the *Lord's Prayer,* commonly called "The Our Father," to illustrate how prepositions *really* work and what they *really* reveal about God's place in, and relationship to, us:

"Our Father who is in heaven…" is more properly and powerfully understood when stated thus: *"My Father who is IN me, WITH me, THROUGH me, BY me, OF me, FOR me, and AS me…."*

"Your kingdom is come, your will is done on earth as it is in heaven…" could be rendered more accurately and assertively thus: *"Your kingdom is come and your will is done IN me, WITH me, THROUGH me, BY me, OF me, FOR me, and AS me, on earth as they* [God's kingdom *and* God's will] *are done* [executed or implemented] *in heaven."*

The Kingdom of God is within you. Enter it and start living life as a ROYAL.

GOD'S LOCATION, POSITION, AND POSE

Do you see what is occurring? We have much more of a relational place and inherent context with God, our Creator, than even the scriptural translations show. The *Lord's Prayer* suddenly becomes more *activated* when seasoned with these prepositions, because the understanding of who we really are is communicated to us with more *intent* and *intimacy* than humankind's traditional translations have ever before allowed.

Instead, traditional scriptures demand an enforced separation from God. How can there be a single-identity relationship and, at the same time, a separation? Adhering to such tragic tradition makes it virtually impossible to experience all the good that is ours by Divine birthright. God deliberately dwells *inside* (another preposition) us, God is excited about that fact, and God wants us to begin and continue an intimate relationship with It. That is one reason the scriptures *correctly* advise us to "In all thy ways acknowledge Him" and "In everything, give thanks."

Even the word "preposition," in this spiritual context, means that God was *pre-positioned*—always and already there—*in, with, through, for, by, of,* and *as* us— *before* the fact of our human creation, existing in unformed and invisible spirit that evolves and expresses itself as (the visible) humankind. How can that be, you ask? Life, which is God, and God, which is life, has no beginning and no ending. It (God) always was, always is, and always will be. How wonderfully these little words—the parts of speech called "prepositions"— perform as they reveal to us this great truth!

You are <u>pre-positioned</u> for success in life because God is, and always will be, pre-positioned in you.

LOOSENING THE GRIP OF ILLUSION

God is everywhere present and is Infinite Energy, Substance, and Divine Intelligence—just to list a few descriptors. Therefore it makes absolutely no sense to continue giving your power to *illusion*—outward circumstances and conditions that are the *effects* of your or somebody else's (inner) thoughts, and that are just as "ill" and "loose" as the word "illusion" seems to describe. You *can* undo conditions, change circumstances, escape a negative environment—all by being committed to doing the *inner work* (in the silent and vast region of pure consciousness) necessary to achieve your goals.

Negative conditions are the "reminders"—the pinches of reality—that prod us into realizing our divinity-identity and recognizing that our life is God's life. We are *one with* God and are *inseparable from* God. It is our oneness with God that is the *wonder* of all creation. Even heaven's angels are employed to do our bidding. Mere conditions disappear when we recognize there is no power behind them, except the direction our thought takes. Redirect the thought and you redirect the condition—away from you or to you, based on your desire and intent.

God WANTS to be found and is easily locatable.
That is why the "search" must begin inside you.

To Be. . . Or Not to Do

Contrary to traditional religious teachings that insist we *do* any number of various and sundry things to *prove* our goodness to God and thus *earn* our place in grace and seats in heaven, all that God requires of us, for the entirety of our human lives, is that we "Be still and know that I am God." All the physical effort required in a lifetime of *doing* is nothing compared to obeying the admonition to "Be still and know that I am God."

While we seek hither and yon for things to *do* in order to ascend the ladder of spirituality, God requires that we not overlook the two most important things: *being still* and *knowing*. God must come first, last, and always. Without the recognition and acceptance of that truth, unwanted or negative conditions persist, given life and permanence by our misunderstanding of, or *our* refusal to recognize, the true Source of our power.

When we recognize that we humans are merely the "vessels" for the in-dwelling and housing of God's spirit, then God responds to us according to this *awareness* of Itself. Each day of our life we are to open our mind and soul and let God express Itself. It is God's mind with which we function and God's breath that we breathe. We would be empty and lifeless statues otherwise. Our recognition of who we are directs how we communicate with God, something we must do frequently. The scriptures (again correctly) advise us to "Pray without ceasing."

You are God in human form and Divine action!

TALKING WITH GOD

You cannot *overpray*. Talk to God daily, several times a day. How? As you would a friend, for God is the best friend we could ever have, for all eternity. Structured thoughts or conversation are not necessary. Speak simply and from the heart. Don't worry about being informal. That is absolutely okay. Say to God: "Here I am, God. Use me for Your good." What a great beginning!

As you continue talking with God, tell It everything (It already knows all about you anyway), and listen— really *listen*—for intuition and insight. Your purpose is to make regular communication with God (via your thoughts or actual words) the tool for *evolving* your human self into a greater understanding and embrace of the God-self within you. Said another way, God cannot *contract* to us. We must, instead, *expand* to God.

We men and women all have the ability to live a God-like life—every single day. How different our human lives would be if we would only accept that we *are* the living essence of the Living God. We are made in the image and likeness of what we know God to be. By opening the door of our mind to accept that truth, the freshness of Spirit flows in—just as the fresh air flows in when, following a vacation, we open the doors and windows of our shuttered house.

Open and keep filled the doorway of your mind with the presence of God.

RECEIVE BLESSINGS EVERY DAY

We must know (through awareness, belief and faith) that every day of our life can be filled with abundant blessings simply by believing and doing what the Great Teacher Jesus commanded us to do: *"Ask and you shall receive, seek and you shall find, knock and it shall be opened up unto you."* The power to live a better, more fulfilling life is in our hands, as regular as our heartbeat, and under our direct control.

There is no need or desire that should remain unfulfilled, no quest that should be fruitless, and no door that should never open to us. We are greater than we know. And knowing and believing this will make us greater than the seeming obstacles, problems, road-blocks, and negative conditions that we face. Problems are seen as teaching-and-learning moments to increase our wisdom and experience. Facing the God within ourselves blesses our lives in so many miraculous and unpredictable ways. By placing God in the center of our lives, we thus put life—true, abundant, spectacular life—back in our days.

> *The rose grows beautifully amidst thorns, its flower and fragrance captivating our imagination. You too are a rose that simply has to be. Don't fight the thorns. Simply BE and GROW. The fragrance of your flower will overcome the problem of any hour.*

YOUR "GREEN APPLE" AFFIRMATION #7

Affirmations are mental and verbal *confirmations* of your total and complete belief in your desires, plans, and goals. We enthusiastically encourage you to say your affirmations repeatedly, daily, *and* meditate on them. It will do you so much good to *hear* your affirmations in your own voice. Meditating on them is like wearing a comfortable, warm, and favorite coat: the feeling is so right.

Meditation is spiritual *medication*. It is your Rx for success and can be powerful and instantly effective. The more you meditate on affirmations and say them, the more you SEE them take form and shape in your life. They are your God-given power to create your world as you wish it to be. Do not underestimate their solid, consistent, and reliable universal power. Remember: *FIRM* is a key part in the word *Affirmation.*

And never forget: *it was with the SPOKEN WORD—affirmation—that God created the heavens and the earth.*

Say and see the following Green Apple:

I praise the power of God in me that frees me to experience a greater level of living. I praise the prospering power of God within me and I welcome my infinite good today. I open my mental eyes and ears to the magnificence of the universe. I am blessed and I have an abundance of every good thing. I share my abundance as I joyously live my life in the expectancy of more good. And so it is.

CHAPTER 8

BORN TO LIVE IN ABUNDANCE

WE WERE BORN in human bodies for a specific and *Divine* reason: to walk and live on this earth plane and—with a spiritual consciousness always attuned to the Divine Presence within us—accomplish great things. We are not human beings on a spiritual journey; rather, we are *spiritual* beings on a human journey. It is Divine Presence that infuses our entire beings and informs us as we fulfill our roles and purposes as humans.

Our relationship to this Divine Presence inside us might better be understood by observing our relationship with our houses and automobiles. Our house or car is *not* us. Such things are merely "containers" that we occupy and control or direct toward specific aims. We sleep in our houses, paint them, and heat them. We drive our cars, wash them, and fill them with gasoline.

Essentially, we can be thought of as the spirit or presence that pervades our homes or automobiles, but we are *not* them and *they* are not us. We might cringe (or at least laugh) if any of our friends or neighbors referred to our house or car by *our name*. By the same token, we are not our bodies, either. Our bodies are physical "containers" that the Divine Presence lives in and controls. We "motor" about with our bodies, exercise them, bathe them, and rest them. But it is the Spirit of the Divine that controls everything in, around, with, and through these self-same bodies.

That Spirit lives in us and expresses its (human) identity *as* us. "*I am created by Divine Mind and am constantly informed by Its Spirit*" is more the attitude to have than the "I'm-only-human" cliché that is all but total misidentification. We are engaged in a human *experience*—by Divine decree. Attuning ourselves to this truth elevates our consciousness and inspires and directs our steps.

> *Your destiny is not in your doing anything—it is in your <u>knowing</u> who you are.*

In Touch and in Tune

You see, our human steps in life are to be placed on the God-trail, the *perfect path* designed expressly for us. Our experiencing—in all its complexity, creativity, and diversity—the many terrains of life on the earth-plane is a unique feat that distinguishes us from angels. As spirit beings, the work of angels is done in the spirit realm. As human spirits made—as the Bible states—"a little lower than the angels," our work is performed specifically in the *physical* realm.

God's work on earth must be done *through* and *as* us. Therefore we must take our cues and information from the Divine Presence that *inspires* us. Angels have their roles, and humans have theirs. Learning to get in touch, and staying in touch, with this Divine Presence is to know truth and, as a consequence, be able to face life without fear: *the Creator of life pronounced it "good" and wants us to be filled with thanksgiving, joy, and faith— not fear.*

We must allow ourselves to be *freely* in touch and in tune with the Divine Presence inside us. That Presence is ignorant about and immune to the "human" obsessions we have: criticisms, social class, culture, economic status, and ethnic background. It is, and has been, eternal; it will always be eternal. It never descends to what we regard as our human plight. Therefore, to surmount our various conditions, we must ascend, in *mind*, to that level of consciousness in our most inner being.

This is what King David meant when he said, "I will lift mine eyes unto the hills from whence cometh my help." *Lifting your eyes* means, in this context, raising your consciousness to seek your innermost being: God. Deliberately *lifting up* your will, your attitude, your desire, your emotions to go "there" and admit, acknowledge, and accept that your "problem" is solved, your desire granted, your wish fulfilled.

> *Ascend to the elevation (the "hills") of the solution—rather than descend to the level of the problem (worries, pains).*

GO INSIDE FOR INSIGHT

The presence of God within us, besides being eternal, is so vast and powerful and eternal that we *literally* have to lift ourselves up from where we are—by taking our

175

attention and emotions completely away from our very temporary "problems" and going inside to commune with the Most High God. This is not an idle pursuit and requires a determined mind, a fixed attitude, and a conscious commitment. One's efforts to hear the voice of God within and be the vessel through which God directs Its energy and purpose are always rewarded when one's *seeking* to find God within is energized by *knowing* that God *is* the answer that is being sought.

The silence that is emphasized in Chapter 7 is an important key that opens the door to the Divine Presence. The Presence *reveals* Itself when we take our attention off the disturbances and distractions in the "external" environment and willingly place our focus onto the universe of silence within us. Asking for the answers we need, and acknowledging that they are already in existence, ensures they become manifest in our experience. The vastness of the universe inside us that God inhabits contains answers for every possible human need—known and unknown.

God's pronouncement of "good" over all Its handi-work includes Its evaluation of us as integral parts of that creation. Contrary to long-held tenets of traditional religion, we were *not* "born in sin and shaped in iniquity." It is we humans, our vision distracted by our legacy of self-imposed problems, who authored that uninspiring, erroneous, and dreadfully pessimistic description of the human condition. That it has been trumpeted for millennia as a religious article of faith shows how long humankind has been in bondage to its own stinking thinking.

God, the Creator, has already revealed the miraculous truth of our Divine origins. We humans, rather than silently (on the inside) acknowledging our Divine heritage, and then (on the outside) demonstrating God in the creation and fulfillment of wondrous works, seem to have been more inclined to wage armed warfare upon ourselves as we blindly sought and still seek to change the world. It is only relatively lately that we seem to be realizing that change in the outer world will come only *after* change is made in the inner world. A well-known Gospel song has, as its famous refrain, "I ain't goin' to study war no more." Alas, we have spent more time, money, misery, and human lives in the pursuit of war!

The art of war is not the art of finding who you are. Inner peace is what you must seek.

WHAT GOD WANTS

God's every desire is for us to experience the *wealth* and *abundance* of Its *entire* creation *everywhere* in Its grand Universe. God's attention is on us—constantly. God purposely chose us to be the physical *vessels* for Its spirit and *emissaries* for expressing Its personality, power, and majesty. As God tells Neale Donald Walsch in *Conversations with God*, when we humans feel love, kindness, generosity, concern, compassion, and joy toward each other, we are expressing God's personality.

God wants to be, and is, *actively* involved in our lives. We *can* and *must* turn away from the millennia-old belief of God as distant, separate, and indifferent and *realize* that God is *us,* and that we are God in human action and interaction. It is our knowing and believing this truth that determines our destiny in life. Outward conditions are but weak and hollow manifestations of inward thoughts. Thoughts repeated and unchanged tend to become beliefs.

Life, then, does to us according to our belief. The Universe gives back to you according to what you believe—regardless of your race, ethnicity, cultural or religious background, or economic status. There are no victims in life, only volunteers: we *volunteer* for poverty rather than prosperity, for suffering rather than healing, for war rather than peace, and for hate rather than love. Unable to face and bear the truth, we conjure up fables about being born at the wrong time, or of the wrong color, or of the wrong gender, or of the wrong religion.

The plain truth is, where we *find* ourselves in life is exactly where we have *taken* ourselves. An old Southern expression declares, "It was his own dog that bit him," meaning the culprit responsible for one's particular difficulties is both known and familiar. Likewise, it is our own beliefs that have "bit" us. Release (let go of) those beliefs, and you will release (cancel) the sting of their bite. No matter how comfortable, or comforting, those beliefs are, they can be a sweet poison that wrecks and takes our very lives. Where you find yourself in your present (temporary) "destination" in life is exactly where you have *arrived,* based on your "transportation": the series of events you created with your beliefs.

> *Life meets you exactly as you meet life: it is you who are both agent and actor upon life's grand stage. Will you applaud or appeal your performance?*

Surpassing Your Past

One of the most important beliefs to get rid of is that you are shackled to the past. Farmers seemingly never tire of telling stories about chickens who watch as their legs are freed of the ropes or metal bands that tether them to the farmyard's hitching post. The farmer cutting off the bands wants the chickens free. But it is his playful making of a well-defined circle, with his finger in the dirt, around the chickens' bodies, that confuses them and leaves them with the very real *belief* that they are still bound. No chicken inside the drawn circle has ever stepped outside it to true freedom. Long after the farmer has gone, the chicken still stands in the circle—trapped and mired in, and immobilized by, its own *past* experience of being shackled. Though the circle is not "real," the chicken's belief about it is *very* real.

Every day gives you an opportunity to *do* more and *be* more. That is why it is important to analyze your beliefs right now. *What "belief-baggage" from any part of your past are you carrying forward into today's life experiences? What truths do you know now that render those beliefs false? Despite their ability to soothe and comfort you, how willing are you to let those beliefs go? Do you realize the sooner you act on (against or counter to) false beliefs—by dropping them—the sooner you become freer?*

Release your false beliefs as soon as you come into the light of truth. Just as you would never eat a meal that is months old, you should never cling to long-held false, destructive, and otherwise negative and unbeneficial beliefs that are swarming with the "bacteria" of age and decay. What you cling to, in terms of your beliefs, clings to you. And like the barnyard chicken deeply convinced it was still chained to the hitching-post, you can be chained to the "hitching-post" of your false and negative beliefs—even in the face of evidence that you are free of them, or that others whom you know are not bound by them. Conversely, when you make the decision to be free of your false beliefs, you *will* be free, despite the arguments and opinions of others to the contrary, or the picture their lives present to you.

Decide to free yourself from your negative thoughts, their shackles and anchors, and their comfort.

GET WHAT YOU EXPECT

In previous pages we discussed the view of the world prior to Columbus' voyage. Just as Columbus was regarded with hostility and suspicion in his day, so was the great mathematician and astronomer Galileo, many years after Columbus. Adding to the personal anguish of his friend Giordano Bruno having been burned at the stake for his cosmological views, Galileo also suffered the public humiliation of having his writings banned by the Pope because he taught that the earth moves around the sun, and not the sun around the earth. Galileo's continual writing and teaching about the wonders and truth of the universe finally landed him in court, where he was tried and forced to recant his views. Following his court trial, he was placed under house arrest and regarded as an enemy of the people.

Yet, the truth of his well-founded belief was eventually proven for all to see. As a result, civilization advanced light-years beyond where it was when he made his world-shaking, "heretical" announcement, just as it had when the comfortable trap of "flat-world" thinking gave way to truth, which Galileo's research strengthened. Sailors no longer feared falling into an oceanic abyss. A highly beneficial consequence of their dropping this false belief was that merchant seamen became wealthy by setting up trading expeditions and sailing into ports they had never known or been to before—because they had never before allowed themselves to sail beyond their "flat-world" fears.

Abundance in all good things ought to be your expectation; your attitude must be that it is your God-given natural lifestyle. In order to achieve it, though, you must realize that any fears you harbor about your achieving prosperity and unlimited good can render you incapable of acquiring the very good that you desire and deserve. Just as animals have the ability to sense fear in human beings, so too do Universal laws *react* to the *presence* of your fears.

Whether you fear that you will *never* have sufficient financial means to take care of yourself and those you love, or whether you feel *guilty* at even the thought of having unlimited prosperity, the result will be the same: it will be extremely difficult for you to accumulate the wealth that is yours by Divine birthright. You cannot acquire wealth and abundance and yet fear that you will *not* do so, any more than you can walk north and south at the same time. You cannot have prosperity and yet feel guilty about it, as though being prosperous were some kind of sin.

You are God's rose, created to bloom on hostile terrain amid the thorns. So bloom!

BROUGHT BY THOUGHT—DIRECTLY TO YOU

Whatever you desire—including wealth and unlimited abundance—is *brought* to you by your *belief* that it *is* yours by Divine decree. You should feel as comfortable about being wealthy and having abundance as you are about being able to breathe, think, walk, and talk. You should also be mindful of the fact that we live in a *mathematical* kind of universe. There are no accidents, only incidents. And *coincidences,* though they may be unexpected, are *not* accidents; they are merely two or more events that occur at or about the *same* time. *"What a coincidence!"* should actually and more accurately be stated, *"What a natural and logical cause and consequence!"*

Nature cannot exist or operate in a vacuum. Whatever happens, occurs by design. "Accident" only means *"I can't ACCEPT IT!"* That is, the *truth* of whatever has occurred is beyond our ability or desire to accept. Universal law, however, is far superior to our wish to be in denial and will not be subordinated to it. It simply continues as is and moves always in the direction of, and according to, Divine order.

Someone once said, "Since you cannot tame time, you must *tell* time." Said another way, the Universe will not change, because it cannot. And God cannot change. It is we who must change—our ideas, habits, thoughts, and practices—and march or "tell time" to the Divine drumbeat. Just as the pace car at the world-famous *Indianapolis 500* auto race sets the race's initial pace (speed and flow), requiring *every* car to get "up to speed," God's spirit inside us is our pace car that instantly and constantly *speaks* to us, from our inner-most being, to get us up to speed with the Divine laws that govern the Universe—and our lives. All we have to do is "go with the flow." That is how we will achieve our Divine purpose.

The Universe works for you, on your behalf, always.
"U" are first in the Universe.

THE "MATHEMATICS" OF THE UNIVERSE

The universe "behaves" according to Divine decree. And it behaves always *for* you. What you think, you eventually experience, as though you specifically *asked* for it. Your "request"—that persistent, powerful repetitious thought—comes back to you as your experience, alive and well. Because we live in a universe that functions with mathematical exactness, what you dwell on—your consistent, concentrated thought—is multiplied.

If you *fear* success and *expect* failure, your constant thought about this is the *seed* that will grow and bloom like a towering tree in the *field* of your experience. *What kind of thoughts are you thinking and what kinds of trees are they planting?* As the legendary automaker and industrial magnate Henry Ford observed, "Whether you think you can [be, do, or have something] or whether you think you cannot, *you are right.*"

Thoughts are powerful. That is a fact you must not ignore or underestimate. Thoughts have an energetic "pull" characteristic of electromagnetic power. The *speed* of thought is the fastest speed known to humans. It is faster than the speed of sound and the speed of light. Remember: you occupy a body only to perform the will and wishes of the Divine Creator. Your real essence—the *essential particle* and *whole* of your being—is MIND. That is why you must both *respect* and *rule* over your thoughts.

Life's great tragedy is that we, instead of spending our days in comfort, too often spend them in "quiet desperation," as the great writer and philosopher Thoreau noted, and as we stated earlier. Are you disappointed about where you are today? Then ask yourself, *"What did I do and how did I complete yesterday?"* Looking at yesterday is a quick reference—a kind of bird's-eye view—that can tell you *how* you *arrived* at where you are today. *Did you establish your will upon life with your thought—and thus know what you're doing today and why—or did you simply arrive at today as the effect of "random" events?*

Life is not meant to be lived in either a helter-skelter or stagnant manner, nor can it be loved or appreciated in those ways. Dynamic thoughts create a dynamic and lovable life. Billionaire Donald Trump made dynamic plans to rescue himself from bankruptcy in the late 1980's. His constant *expectation* that he would succeed resulted in his *experiencing* a spectacular comeback. Danielle Steel, the internationally renowned novelist, *expected* to get twenty-six (26) parking permits from her local city council, for her family and friends to visit her at her palatial estate in the San Francisco area. Despite notoriously scarce parking—a situation that limited most permit awards to two per household—Ms. Steel received precisely what her *dynamic* expectations ordered; and she entertains as many people as she wishes in regal splendor and abundance.

God in you—that Divine Presence which created life everywhere and the heavens and earth in which that life abounds—operates for you by calling forth from the storehouse of the Universe whatever you need.

VICTIM OR VICTOR?

It is not important what happens *to* you—what happens *in* you is all that matters: the kind of internal response you make. You can reverse any circumstance that has happened *to* you and make it something *for* you. Your spiritual compass and your intimate connection to God-in-you need not be disturbed at all, at any time, or for any reason. Thus you can move *yourself* from a position of *victim* and assume the posture of the *victor.*

If you choose to stay on the floor of your mind as a victim, and blame others or "the system" for your fate, failures, and circumstances, then life will continue to grant and confer upon you "victimhood." If, however, you choose to lift your eyes to the hills from whence comes your help and reach forth toward the *summit* of your mind, life will grant you the throne of the triumphant *victor.*

Royal living comes from royal thinking. With this in mind, it is vital that you understand there is no such thing as *not* thinking. Some people believe that when they sleep they are not thinking. However, the mind does not work that way. It is *always* thinking—far beyond our ability to fully comprehend how or why. Even when you do not think, you are making a *mental choice* not to engage in thought; thus, you have to think that you will *not* think.

Since the mind is always active and never stops thinking, you must feed it only right and positive and productive and loving thoughts. If thoughts of love, abundance, and good occupy your mind, then you will have love, abundance, and good. The Universe functions with mathematical exactness to give *back* to you what you first give to it as thought.

God created you to thrive, not merely survive. As evidence of God's desire that *all* of its creation thrive, just look around you. Ask yourself: Can I count the number of rays in the sunlight? The number of oxygen particles in the air? The leaves on a tree? The capillaries and arteries in my body? The veins in the husk on an ear of corn? The gallons of water in the ocean? The atoms in the atmosphere? The number of sand grains on the beach? Of course not. All this is impossible.

God's will that Its life live and move in complete and constant abundance is so richly evident that we simply cannot limit how life thrives in our midst by trying to assign a *number* to the phenomenon known as creation. The sun lives and thrives in all its brilliance. And so, too, are we to live—by thriving. When babies are first born, the hospital birthing center personnel are instantly attuned to whether the babies are thriving or merely "hanging on." A thriving baby gets hungry and cries loudly to ensure it gets fed. It notices its strange surroundings and takes active interest in them. Its seeming restlessness and agitation are all part of its thriving "introduction" to its environment.

However, when a newborn begins to just "hang on" and demonstrates no interest in its surroundings and is indifferent about being fed or nurtured, it is in the grip of something that is not healthy but is counter to nature. *Are you like a thriving "newborn" or like a baby merely surviving and hanging on?*

Decide to thrive and the Universe will come alive with the "sound" of your decision.

SECURITY COMES FROM CONSCIOUSNESS, NOT CONDITIONS

Changing or failing (outward) conditions, to which we have long accustomed ourselves, can delude us into thinking that our security itself is threatened. Nothing could be further from the truth. And it is only because of our mis-education that we place our faith in our outer conditions. Remember: outward conditions are merely the effects of inward thinking. They are the *demonstrated* result or *picture* of our inner thoughts at work. Conditions change because they are *not* secure, that is, permanent. However, our faith need not rise or fall with every change of condition.

Placing our faith in conditions is having "other gods before me," a taboo the Bible warns us against. It is not for God's benefit or glory that we are issued such a warning, but for *our* benefit. Why? It is impossible to maintain and sustain your mental, emotional, physical, and spiritual security by anchoring them to circumstances and conditions that, because they are *effects*, necessarily *must* change: for example, the stock market; the cost of living index and the value of money; a peace-time or war-time economy; or the significance of racial, ethnic, and cultural background.

Your security is God. Your *knowing* that God is working in and through you, and your awareness of

God's hand in all your affairs, is your unshakable connection to God. Your total at-oneness with God is your security. God will never fail you. God is the same yesterday, today, and forevermore. God always is. And if you are to be secure, you must always be *there* with God.

The wonder of life and all the beauty and rich abundance that life contains are gifts that are promised to us in the biblical directive: "Seek ye first the kingdom of God and all these things shall be added unto you." Just as the sun has to come out first to take the chill off the air, whereupon the dew evaporates and returns to the heavens, we must also approach life with a *first things first* attitude. Our first and ever-always "marching orders" are to seek first the kingdom of God. That means we must have the *consciousness* that we are directly and divinely connected *to* God—not to social circumstances or world events. It is that consciousness that God is the Answer, the Healer, the Giver, that brings us into the wonderful realm of *possibilities*—precisely the environment defined by the Master Teacher Jesus' utterance: "All things are possible if you only believe."

And ALL has been created by God for our enjoyment and fulfillment. Astronauts in press interviews have said that when they returned to earth after rocketing to the moon, their lives were altered forever. The vast unknown called "outer space" taught the astronauts a thing or two about God and changed their thinking. Yet we do not have to go to outer space to know, respect, trust, believe, and obey God. The world that is inside us is more vast and complex than any geographical or stratospheric region outside ourselves. The same God who made the solar system, constellation, and galaxies made us, and dwells in us.

Our consciousness of this truth is—in astronaut talk—our "mission control." And like astronauts, we must "touch down." But instead of merely returning to earth, we must return to our *Divine worth*. Or, as the world-renowned musician Chick Corea states, "Return to forever." Being merely "in orbit"—connected to and controlled by events outside ourselves—can drain our energies, pull us away from our God-Source and, of course, alter our spiritual consciousness. By going inside and communing, in silence, with the Most High God, we can make the safest "return" imaginable.

The content of your "inner space" determines your contentment in "outer space: your family, society, the world at large."

LOVE, THE TRUTH BEHIND EVERYTHING

With our hearts and minds embracing this wonderful truth, it is, therefore, impossible for us to fail to live a God-directed, abundant, and productive life. It is this truth that sets us free. And the more our attention is attuned to the Divine Presence within us, the freer we continuously become. Problems disappear before our very eyes, and the illusion that sustained them in the first place vanishes. As your attention to the Presence of God within you develops, and your consciousness is strengthened, you will see—really see—the truth behind all things. If something is not based in truth, you will find yourself wanting nothing to do with it.

You will like the "new" you as you continue to grow spiritually, and you will develop a deeper understanding and appreciation of those around you. Why? Each person houses the Divine Presence within him/herself. That is why the scriptures instruct us to love our neighbors as ourselves. That is also why the Great Teacher Jesus said to "Love your enemies, bless them that curse you, do good to them that spitefully use you."

The power of love is the greatest power ever known, and it is yours to use. You can never *overuse* your power to love. So use it freely (for example, a kind word, a blessing, an inspirational note, a hug, a kiss, a touch, a compliment, a listening ear showing your concern), and watch the conditions around you change for the better.

It is not the love of force but the force of love that improves and enhances all life.

BELIEFS: BARRIERS OR BLISS

The barriers to such a grand and exalted life are those which we erect with our own thinking. There are no other barriers. The Great Teacher Jesus walked on water, turned water into wine, and rose from his grave after three days to show us that all things—literally *all* things—are possible. Belief is both the fuel and the force that transforms the possibilities into realities.

Your belief can take you anywhere. That is precisely why it is important to know *what* you believe: you want to make sure you are where you *want* to be. Where you are right now, and what you are experiencing, is a direct outgrowth of the "bank account" of the accumulated beliefs you have been "depositing." You are now collecting the "interest" on those beliefs, in the form of your present condition or experience. *Do you like your present experience? Do you want more of your circumstances or less of them?* Whatever your answer is, THE ultimate answer is: change your life for the better by changing your beliefs. You will get exactly what you desire. Change your mind...and keep the change.

What is God's agenda for you? To "Be still and know that I am God." What a simple and frank and powerful command! Humanity has been everything but "still" and, as a consequence, the drama of human life is plagued with all kinds of tragedies. There is no fiction that could compare with the true story and actual events of human history as we have slipped, slid, swaggered, staggered, muttered, murdered, stalked, stolen, walked, and wasted on life's great stage. In a word, we have done it all. But alas, in our march through history, we have taken ourselves *away* from the Divine.

There is a genre of dramatic playwriting called "absurdist drama." In this genre, the characters in a play do all sorts of strange and incredible things. Absurdist drama was developed on the premise that humankind, separated from God and alienated from themselves (their family, society, and their personal selves) would drift and become engaged in all sorts of deranged and absurd behaviors. The point is: *arrange* your life in and with God. Otherwise, the consequences of a *deranged* life can be too great to bear.

It is God's good pleasure to give us the kingdom. God's faith in us is total and complete. Yet our faith in

God often falters or fails utterly, as we let our attention get "hijacked" by external appearances and effects. With one's mind so flooded by negative news accounts and appearances of scarcity, war, lack, and limitation, it is little wonder that one's faith is invested in failure and one's belief system is built on defeat. Life cares little for outward appearances of poverty and lack, or the individuals overcome by them. In fact, because life is always meeting us at the level of our awareness, one's defeatist attitude and failure-consciousness only brings one more of the same: defeat and failure.

As we have already observed, there are no victims in life, only volunteers. We all *volunteer* for the positions we assume and the roles we play in life. While blind to outward appearances and effects, we must grasp the tie that binds us to the Divine Presence within. Sending to the Universe thoughts of abundance, constant good, joy, love, and thanksgiving is the fail-proof way for receiving these gifts in your experience. Life cannot meet us at a point higher than our consciousness. So grow in faith, rather than grousing about conditions; and reach *for* life, don't retreat *from* it. Thus you will build the consciousness that *commands* life to give you all that you desire and deserve.

> *Your life follows your consciousness. As your consciousness goes, so goes your life.*

WHOSE LIFE IS IT ANYWAY?

Life never stands still, it never goes backwards, and it never lingers. But we humans do all these things and, in exasperation, we exclaim, "That's life!" Nothing could be further from the truth. Life is dynamic and is constantly changing. Too many of us, though, are only crying and constantly complaining. The Master Teacher Jesus taught that "the Kingdom of Heaven is at hand." He meant that heaven is available to us and opens up its good only when we open our consciousness to the God-in-us.

The power to open up our consciousness is, figuratively speaking, in our hands—*"at hand."* You live life according to the thoughts, ideas, and habits you have established. Expand your consciousness and awareness of the unlimited good all around you, and build into your mind only solid God-ideas. See the truth inside yourself by recognizing and rejoicing in the God-in-you. Today, right now, decide to stop looking for the truth *outside* of yourself—it will only move farther and farther away.

Realize that you have—through Jesus the Christ's teachings, exemplary life, and assurance—all that you desire. Therefore, approach prayer and meditation with *thanksgiving* for your blessings—present and future—that you already have. Recognize and realize that the power and presence of God are working in you to bring about all that is necessary to fulfill your desires. You can only know this by going *within* to your vast, silent consciousness and meditating. God in you becomes your Guide and, through you, exerts perfect control over your life. Your acceptance of this truth enables you to become your own agent through whom God works, to do *for* you what you cannot do for yourself.

The good life, one that produces all the rich blessings and abundance that you desire, has to be lived on the God-plane. That is because life is a creation of

Spirit. It is impossible to achieve or acquire, through *human* means, what only the Spirit—working through you—will grant to you. Prayer and meditation are your tools for rendering your entire life to God's purpose and power. What you get, in return, is tremendous control over your life and the vision and ability to create and invent it exactly as you want it.

Placing your life in God's hands puts the Kingdom of Heaven in your hands.

How Do You See Life?

God is totally and completely incapable of creating anything less than what God is. Then why is it that we do not see ourselves as we truly are? It is because we have not developed the habit—again, through constant prayer and meditation—of seeing life through God's eyes. That means you must consciously visualize your life the way you want it to be. You can no longer use your eyes merely for seeing life on the outside and subjecting yourself to its effects and their control over you.

You must commune with the Divine Presence within you and *create* the ideal picture of your life and *project* it, from within, through your lens. Build these pictures with your thoughts: think about the kind of life you want. Be excited about your thoughts in this regard. Then see yourself being, doing, and having all those wonderful things you want in your good life. As Ernest Holmes, the founder of the teaching known as Religious Science, states in his book *The Science of Mind,* the life of God is in us—*as* us.

Just as a movie-theater projectionist places the film in the projector and transforms a huge, blank screen into a wonderful, dynamic, and scenic canvas, you too must install the "film" resulting from your praying and meditating: beam your life's ideal picture through your eyes, and practice *seeing* it on the canvas of your experience. Soon, sight and sense (of expectation) will become one, and your pictured life will become your real experience.

The good life will come to you with practice. Learn to see the world as *you* are—beautiful, magnificent, successful, Divine. Thus, through the law of "like attracts like"—a magnetic force—you will attract the people, events, and circumstances to you that will aid and assist you in making your intended and envisioned good life a living reality. Edit your thoughts and curb your negative thinking. Your seeing the world as *you* are –rather than as *it* appears to be—allows those people in the world to see you all the more clearly and come to help you remake your life.

The amount of control such thinking and seeing places in your hands is, well...*heavenly*. As stated previously, heaven is a state of mind, not a place. Life is as beautiful as the light you let into your eyes allows you to envision it. Let more "light" into your eyes by purposely blessing and being thankful for all the beauty around you *and* in you. As you exult over the magnificent oceans, the waves crashing, the force and fury of the winds, don't forget to thank God for *your* own wonderfulness. Looking at life is a vital exercise in learning to look back on—and into—ourselves. Just as Lake Erie is the force behind the breath-taking Niagara

Falls, God is the Force and Source behind *us*. It is our Cause and Reason for being. We are God's expression, Its physical utterances: God spoke and we became.

An instructive fable says that one day the sun was eavesdropping on some visitors who were talking about their visit to the darkest planet they had ever seen. So shaken were they by their visit that they could not stop talking about it. Curious, the sun went to investigate, searching far and wide for this strangely dark planet. Finally, it arrived at the planet only to find that it was not dark—anymore.

The lesson is: the biblical scriptures tell us we are the *light* of the world. And wherever there is light, there is truth. Knowing the real truth of *who*—not just *what*—we are is the all-powerful light that illuminates the abundant good that God has prepared for us *and* casts out all darkness (problems and negative conditions, including people).

> *God's inner light, shining through you, illuminates your outer life.*

RECEIVING AND GIVING: ONE AND THE SAME

In addition to training your mind, heart, and entire being to believe in the God-Presence in you *because* it *is* you in whom God believes, you need to understand the workings of a particular "power point" in *bringing* to you the good that you desire. *Giving* is the power that causes your good to be transmitted *back* to you—the receiver. Receiving good cannot be fully or reliably achieved without your giving good. Moreover, what you receive is in direct proportion to how and what you give. The principle of giving and receiving works just like breathing: you cannot *receive* a breath until you *give* a breath. Again, in life you receive in proportion to what you give.

The author Stretton Smith, in his book *The 4T's: Time, Tithe, Talent, and Treasure,* identifies these four areas (composing the book's title) as crucial channels through which to give. Think of time, tithe, talent, and treasure as a kind of four-lane highway. When you give in these areas, you are giving God away. Since God is inexhaustible, your good comes right back to you—by making a U-turn constantly.

You always receive through the same size "hole" through which you give. The ultimate truth is that when you give, you are giving to yourself! The scriptures state that "It is better to give than to receive." The reason is that giving is the power point for receiving. *You* are that power. And that is the ideal position. However, if you are in the position of receiving from others, because you are unable or have nothing to give, that is an unfortunate, undesirable, and disadvantageous position in which to be. Giving is the essence of independence; receiving—being a dependent recipient—is a shameful position the poor and ignorant associate with "bad luck."

> *Decide to be a giver in life, and life will give back to you to your heart's content.*

197

Reaping/Sowing; Action/Reaction; Cause/Effect

The mind is like a magnet. It draws to you what you focus on the most. As the saying goes, "Whatever has your attention, *has* you." What we focus on and give our thought energy to always comes back to us as an experience. Remember: the scriptures state, "It is done unto you as you believe." And the experiences that confront us are as though we decreed them. Indeed, "It is done unto you as you *decree*" very accurately describes the nature and quality of our thought energy. It works as a command, *decreeing* the resultant experiences that become our fate.

When the biblical Job cried out in anguish, "The thing I feared most has come upon me!" he was confessing to being trapped in the prison of his own fear-tormented thinking. What he *thought* up, he *brought* up—into his real-life experience. The loss of his wife and family, as well as his friends and fortune, was the effect of fastening his thought and emotions on fears that he continued to fertilize time and again, until he faced a hideous harvest—a "bumper crop" of plagues the likes of which he had *always* (by his own admission) imagined!

The God-Presence within us desires deeply—beyond our ability to understand—that we accept, acknowledge, and appreciate how wondrously Divine we truly are. There is no other element of God's creation that It proudly displays and declaims as being made "in Our Image." Think of the eternal pride with which our Creator proclaims that, in Genesis, the very first book of the Bible! Our accepting the truth that we are made in the image and likeness of God and, further, that the Mind of God is our Mind, will ignite the spiritual energy (*engine*) necessary for bringing (and keeping) our good to us, in constant, abundant supply.

Our being made in the image and likeness of God means this: we are God in action, living in the *form* of humans. We are more God than we are human. As we saw earlier, our "humanness" is merely a shell that covers the Spirit that inspires, instructs, and directs us.

Our natural state is beauty, life, love, wealth, bigness. Yet we see life in small terms. Life, then, "pays" us according to our *expectations*. As you consider this word *expectations*, think of the word *spectacles*. Spectacles are eyeglasses: aids for improving sight. What you *see*—expect—is exactly what you receive: you *re-see* it as your experience. Enhance your vision (by expanding your belief), broaden your expectations, and increase and dramatically improve your experience.

How many people do you know who fuss and fume about a particular circumstance by blurting out, "Just as I thought!" or "Yeah, I knew it was never going to be!" or even "Why am I *not* surprised?!" They sowed the seeds of bad thought and plowed the field that later bloomed into the experience to which they mightily objected. It is much better to be passionate and positive in the very beginning—infusing your thoughts with optimism and confidence and positive expectations—than to be ranting and raving at the end, and crying, "Poor me!"

You are the sower of life's seed. Your planted thoughts either make you your own jailer or they make you free.

CAUSE AND EFFECT

Jesus was the only person (as a human) who could silence the chatter of his "outer mind." He knew, in advance, the outcome of his hopes and dreams because he had the required faith and belief. All that he allowed into his mind was his confidence, determination, and belief that his prayers would result in his desire being granted. Whether he was healing the sick or raising the dead, it was *his belief* that brought about the phenomena we have come to call "miracles."

That is why it is *how* you pray and meditate and *what* you believe that brings your result to you, or to those you care about. Thought, energized by prayer and meditation, knows no distance, limitation, geography, space, or time. Thought is pure, creative power and *changes the mind of the thinker/prayer*. It is *your* faith that makes you, the situation you're encountering, or a loved one or friend in need whole and healed. You must properly understand your role in this *cause-and-effect/action-reaction* characteristic of prayer, faith, and healing. What you think and how you pray is all that matters. It is not important what the other person, who needs the healing, thinks, or what the "history" of those external conditions or situations is.

Finding the faith that is greater than your fears is exactly how you can save your own spiritual life. And it is precisely this vital activity—finding that faith—that you must practice. Exercise your faith; it is like a muscle, a machine, a tool to be used. The more you use it, the stronger it becomes. There are no limits to the growth and dimension of your faith. Faith is the sphere (as in *atmosphere*) that must *surround* your entire life, and *every* aspect of it. Faith and belief are forces that fear *cannot* withstand or conquer. Face life with faith and life will face you back with rich and abundant rewards.

Your imagination and what you envision become the engine that transports your experience to you.

YOUR "GREEN APPLE" AFFIRMATION #8

Affirmations are mental and verbal *confirmations* of your total and complete belief in your desires, plans, and goals. We enthusiastically encourage you to say your affirmations repeatedly, daily, *and* meditate on them. It will do you so much good to *hear* your affirmations in your own voice. Meditating on them is like wearing a comfortable, warm, and favorite coat: the feeling is so right.

Meditation is spiritual *medication*. It is your Rx for success and can be powerful and instantly effective. The more you meditate on affirmations and say them, the more you SEE them take form and shape in your life. They are your God-given power to create your world as you wish it to be. Do not underestimate their solid, consistent, and reliable universal power. Remember: *FIRM* is a key part of the word *Affirmation*.

And never forget: it was with the SPOKEN WORD—affirmation—that God created the heavens and the earth.

Say and see the following Green Apple:

Today I am thankful for the light of truth that shines within me. Every day of my life is filled with God's love and abundance. I am grateful for all that I have received and I look forward with great anticipation to even greater blessings. My life is rich beyond compare. In me and through me God has created heaven here on earth now. Each moment of my life is a gift from God. I affirm the presence of God everywhere. I keep my mind open to Divine guidance and am happy to know that everything good is mine, in this moment. And so it is.

YOUR CALL TO ACTION

GOD'S *LITTLE GREEN APPLES* are yours for the picking. They are always ripe and sweet, eternally in season, and waiting for you. You could feast on them forever, for you stand in the most spacious, splendid, and magnificent apple orchard in the Universe. This book, by helping you to realize your *Divinity-Identity*, will also help you to achieve your life's purpose according to God's plan. *Today,* it is up to you to take action. You must *do* something with the vital truths and concepts you have read in this book.

Picking the *"green apples"*—following the recommendations below—will place and keep you on the path to ever-abundant and lifelong success. Whether you reach above your head for the green apples, or whether they fall at your feet, you *must* do the *picking*. It is only then that you can "bite into" (have) your new and changed experiences. God's green-apple tree will always be in the orchard of your life. Pick quickly and pick continuously. Start now!

● Greet each day by first greeting the God within you. Thank God for granting you a brand new day in which to live. Ask God, as the Australian Aborigines are said to do daily, to "show me your will for me, in the wonder and splendor of today."

- Approach life like the successful and wealthy gold prospectors. "Prospect" means to go forth and find that which you envision. "Pro" means to support or represent, and "spect" means view or sight. So, *prospecting* means going and doing that which supports your vision.

- Rid yourself of any false beliefs that life is meant to be difficult and that you must endure some suffering in order to really appreciate any blessings you expect to receive. Instead, go forth and *claim* your good. Take the scriptures literally when they quote God as saying, "Command thou me!" *Tell* God exactly what you want and go out and get it. Your good awaits you but will come to you only when you realize and believe that inside you is an infinitely loving God who is so very thoughtful that It has arranged for you to *order* the good into your life.

- Banish guilty thoughts or feelings of suspicion about your accumulating good, by being ceaselessly thankful for it.

- Life cannot be limited, so don't even try. If you do, life will only limit you back. So, live life to the fullest—in full faith—and be fulfilled.

- Count your blessings and watch them multiply. Use this *blessing* exercise: bless the "less" and "sing" your gratitude and life's praises for the *more* that comes to you.

- Start each day with positive, pure, and productive thoughts. Keep this up throughout the day, seeing yourself always as a ray of sunlight that simply beams and beams and beams—everywhere.

- Break the habit of negative thinking. Realize that you are the thinker who thinks the thoughts that shape your life. Thoughts, like clay, are meant to be shaped. So, make new "molds" for your thoughts. And change the molds as often as you wish. There is absolutely no limit to the size of your molds or the frequency with which you change them. Let each mold serve your purposes—that is, to make positive and progressive growth—and let it be the "mode of transportation" that takes you to your next success.

- Realize that you are constantly "writing," "producing," and "directing" the story of your life. Whatever "picture" life is playing back to you, *you* wrote the script for it. If you don't like this picture, you need to write, produce, and direct a new script. Change your life by changing your *life-script.*

- Stay in touch, in tune, and united with the God in you. Thus you are consciously and constantly unified with the answer to all your needs. Live in the solution, not in the problem.

- Be generous with your love as the Universe is generous with you. Love, the most potent spiritual force, is a healer and a balm that takes away all pain. Let God's pure and free love channel through you as the sunlight filters through the clouds. Make your rainbow seen everywhere.

- Have high goals. Stretch forth and reach toward them as though you were plucking the highest and sweetest fruit from the tree. Low goals require no real energy and simply do not take you very far. Remember: You *go* where your goals are.

- Live from the highest mountains of your thought. Do not descend into the valley of victimhood. Constantly upgrade your thinking and watch your life become upgraded.

- Acknowledge that the good you seek already exists. Then *live* in the constant expectation of receiving it.

- Talk to the God-in-you constantly with your thoughts. Make this a habit. Don't wait until a special day, such as a regular day of worship, to do this. God lives in you because It wants you to communicate with It. So communicate, don't procrastinate.

- Guard the door of your mind and the gateway of your mouth. Pay strict attention to what you think, and think only good, clean, pure, and profitable thoughts. That which you think becomes your word. Watch your word because it becomes your action. Watch your action because it becomes your habit. Watch your habit because it shapes your character. Watch your character because it makes your destiny.

- Know that in this journey called life, your faith is the fuel that ignites the engine of your belief that drives you in either the garbage truck or the limousine of your destiny. So watch *where* and in *what* you place your faith, for your faith leads to your fate!

● The Bible says that your word "is made flesh." That means it is your word that makes *real* ("flesh") your experience. Take great care to say only good words that come from good thoughts, and do not judge others. What you say is what you *pay* in the boomerang effect of experience. Put another way, words *save* or words *slay*.

● Meditate daily, at least three times a day. Meditation is spiritual *medication* that connects you with your Higher and Healing Power. Prayer can be described as talking to God, and meditation as *listening* to God.

● Decide that your mind is a castle, not a casket; a tower, not a tomb. Control the thoughts you allow inside it, for they will either frustrate you and fence you in, or free you. Climb the ladder of live and liberating thoughts. Never ally yourself with mummified, "stinking thinking." Constantly think new and different thoughts.

● Know that you were born to bring God into full expression in and through your life. You are not— nor have you ever been—alone. Build a fortress-like, impenetrable consciousness around the truth that God works for you by working *with* and *in* you.

● Your mind was created to be attuned to the energy of the entire Universe. Your mind is light-years more than what lies between your ears. Therefore, do not limit your thinking. Instead, know that you *think* with the unlimited power and energy of God, with whom you are *united*. God cannot be limited and can only grant you what your thought-consciousness has expanded to and embraced. This relationship can be thought of as a principle of expansion-and-contraction: God cannot *contract* (reduce) to you; therefore, you must *expand* (grow) to God.

- Take charge of your emotions and realize that you are a part *of* God, not apart *from* God. Know in your quiet, undisturbed consciousness that your Creator-God lives inside you and deliberately "partners" with you to ensure your success, despite outward appearances.

- The only time you have is *NOW.* Do not worry about yesterday or fret about tomorrow. Yesterday was "now" when it was here; tomorrow will be "now" when it appears. So, concentrate your thought and energies on *now: today, the present time. Now* is all there is. Live in the now. Do not be a "wish-fit," caught between wishing yesterday had never been and tomorrow would never come.

- Stay "prayed up"—make prayer a daily, constant practice. Know that prayer changes your mind—not God's mind. You are the special ingredient that, when *changed,* adds—like salt—to the Universe's "recipe" for your life. It is *your* will to change that causes the wheels of life to roll *for* you.

- Develop a *giving* consciousness and thus overcome lack and limitation. The more you give, the more you receive; that is the law of the Universe. Giving and receiving are the same thing—opposite sides of the same yardstick. Your wealth flows to and through you, *activated* by God *in* you. You cannot beat God at giving, nor can you out-give the wealth that God imparts to and through you. So give and live abundantly.

- Always look around you and *count* your good—a powerful exercise for improving your vision. Think, know, and live positively. You are a majority of ONE, instantly and intimately connected to God. This is what makes humans so *"ONE-derful."* Our unified and eternal connection to God is *wonderful* for all God's creation to behold!

- Release and let go of things that are not working *for* you. If allowed to remain, they can add pollutants that drain energy from your life. Use your power to decide what stays in and what goes out of your life. Remember: it is *your* life.

- Practice the habit of forgiveness. Since life is always *for* you—including *everything* that happens *to* you—absolutely no one can stop you, hurt you, or hold you back. So, forgive and bless that/those person(s) and move on. Consciously do this when you pray and meditate. And consciously *request* the Universe to forgive *you* for any hurts, disappointments, and betrayals you may have caused. Forgiveness is both freedom and pure power. It is like a special fuel additive that launches your life's rocket like nothing else can.

- Just as you give more time and energy to the flowers and *not* the weeds in your garden, you should constantly focus on and live in the *energy* of the solution to the seeming problem. Thus the problem disappears for lack of attention and care.

- Never look back, for, as the great baseball player Satchel Paige said, "something might be gaining on you." Always have a forward-looking attitude. It is the Christ Consciousness of knowing that "greater things than I do, you shall also do" that gives you the *competence* to acquire all the abundant good your heart desires. You need never look back. Keep your mind's *gear* in "Drive," not "Reverse."

- Know and believe what the Master Teacher Jesus declared: "All that the Father has is yours." Just as the food is already stocked for us on our supermarket's shelves—ours, literally, for the taking—*all* the good that God has prepared for us is *ready* and *waiting* for us to acknowledge and accept it for our lives.

- Practice the "attitude of gratitude." Be like Jesus, who always lifted his eyes (consciousness) to the hills and expressed his thanks to God the Father, *knowing* that his need was already fulfilled. You *must* have this kind of knowing, for it is this sort of *faith* that establishes its *dominance* over your life.

- Silently bless the presence of God in everyone you meet: "*The presence of God in me salutes and blesses the presence of God in you.*" The electrostatic "current" you thus set in motion will be felt by others, and they will give glory to the God in themselves.

- Realize that it is the God-light that glows within you, and let it shine, shine, and shine. *Meet and greet and go with this glow!*

- Decide to be a *victor* and not a victim. Realize that it is *you* who deal life's cards. If you do not like the cards you are holding, re-shuffle the deck. If you still do not like your "hand," get a new deck.

- Travel on your own path and live for your own destiny, not somebody else's. Know your mind, trust your heart, and take your own course in life—not somebody else's.

- Always know that God is in you. The larger question then becomes: *Where are you?*

- You are greater than you know; otherwise, God would not have invested Its time and energy to create you. Accept your God-ness and soar to the heights of the unprecedented success you were meant to have.

- Recognize that there is no power in outward appearances. These "external effects" are the byproducts of thought. And that is where the *correction effort* must take place: in thought. *You bring it because you think it. If you brought it up, it is because you thought it up.* Decide to change your thinking and thereby change your experience.

- You can do only what your level of awareness enables you to do. Like the eagle, your strength lies in your vision. So, increase your level of awareness—by increasing your faith in and acceptance of God's already-prepared blessings for you—and thus increase your life's "strengths" (success and prosperity).

- Know that the Divine Presence within you reveals Itself to you when you take your mind off "external distractions" and turn within. So turn within constantly. Stop giving your power to these external distractions and outward appearances.

- Realize that you were born to live in abundance, not in abandonment. Decide to blossom like the rose, shine like the sun, and let wealth into your life like a mighty river.

- Know that God's attention is always on you—you are Its most favored creation.

- Know that life gives you (back) what you give life. Give only the best and highest good.

- Realize that the Universe is friendly and operated *for* you, 24 hours a day, 365 days per year—forever. Plant your good thoughts back into the Universe and reap an abundant and constant harvest of good in all areas of your life.

- Be a high-level, high-grade being, constantly in tune with the Divine Presence within you. Guard your time and keep your presence *away* from individuals whose consciousness "vibrates" at lower levels, as evidenced by their gossip and criticisms, their jealous comments, their in-the-gutter opinions, and their nagging negativism. As Solomon says in the scriptures, "He [or she] who remains in the company of the wise, shall be made wise, but the companion of fools shall be destroyed."

- Look at yesterday only to determine how you arrived at where you are today. Take a "page" out of the book of yesterday to use as a blueprint for change and continued success.

- Know and accept that the content of your "inner space" determines your *contentment* in "outer space."

- Arrange your life *in* and *with* God. That is your guarantee for spectacular success and avoiding a deranged, destitute, frustrating, and unsatisfying life experience.

- What you have your attention on, also has *its* attention on you. Focus the power of your attention only on what you truly desire. Do not leave your attention "on idle," *unattended,* or on "auto-pilot," picking up both trash and treasure on its "screen."

- You must recognize and accept that you are created by God in Its image and likeness. You are both divinity *and* royalty. Rise up and *own* your throne, and rule life from inside your royal court!

A TRIBUTE TO
REV. DR. O.C. SMITH

Ocie Lee Smith, Jr. was born in Mansfield, Louisiana to Ocie Lee Smith, Sr. and Ruth Edwards Shorter. When he was ten, his parents, who were teachers, moved to Little Rock, Arkansas. Three years later, O. C. Smith moved with his mother to Los Angeles and attended Jefferson High School, where he played football and was active on the school swim team. Most important, during his teen years he truly loved singing at parties and performing at school social events.

O. C. Smith attended East Los Angeles Junior College and then returned to his roots in Louisiana to attend Southern University in Baton Rouge, majoring in psychology. O. C. would tell you with a smile, "This was not a bad preparation for life in show business." Following college, he joined the Air Force and Special Services as an entertainer on military bases all over the world. Once his 'hitch' was over, he headed for New York and a full-time career as a singer.

O. C. worked in clubs in New York in the winter and the legendary 'Borscht Belt' hotels in the Catskills in the summer, waiting for the 'big break' that would make the difference. One day at a local hangout for struggling young entertainers, he learned that Count Basie was looking for a replacement for 'the' Joe Williams. For the next three years he toured with Count Basie, developing a huge national following. He left Basie for a solo career and his monumental hit, "Little Green Apples."

O. C.'s life as a singer had the flow and tempo of a hit song that finds its audience and never lets it go. He received a Grammy nomination for his million-copy-selling standard, "Little Green Apples." The song itself was a Grammy winner and has since been designated one of the "Songs of the Century" by the American Society of Composers, Authors and Publishers (ASCAP).

O. C. followed that hit with "Hickory Holler's Tramp" and the following year's "Daddy's Little Man." He sang the theme songs for the motion pictures "The Learning Tree" and "Shaft's Big Score," and he racked up more hit records with "Help Me Make It through the Night," "For the Good Times," "That's Life," "Don't Misunderstand," "Dreams Come True" and "What Cha Gonna Do."

At the height of his musical career, O. C. Smith recognized the need to contribute to humanity. With the increase of violence and crime, he recognized the need for spiritual healing in the world. It didn't take much effort, because he naturally generated love, peace, and happiness in everything he did. He immersed himself in years of study until he emerged as a minister of Religious Science.

Rev. Dr. O. C. Smith was ordained in January of 1985 under the guidance of Dr. Frank Richelieu, Minister of Redondo Beach Church of Religious Science. He dedicated his life to the teachings that he believed in and mastered. 'The Rev,' as he was known by his friends and members, had a special gift and used his skills as he touched everyone with his love, music, generosity, counseling, and his incredible method of teaching people about life. He lived the principles of Religious Science long before he became a minister.

In September of 1985, Rev. Dr. O. C. Smith and his wife, Robbie, sent out stylish invitations to hundreds of friends, fellow-entertainers, and acquaintances, asking them to join in celebrating the opening and first service of the new City of Angels Science of Mind Center at The Proud Bird's Grand Ballroom. The invitation promised "An Abundance of Music and the Spoken Word."

The mailing list looked like a veritable Who's Who in entertainment, sports, business, and politics. On October 13, 1985 nearly three hundred people arrived for the debut. Robbie transformed the ballroom at The Proud Bird into a haven for music, meditation, and homage to the spirit within. By request of the members, the church opened its doors for midweek services. They requested classes and seminars to learn more of the concepts and practices of the Science of Mind.

In October 1985, Rev. Dr. O. C. Smith established the City of Angels Children's Charities and Scholarship Foundation. The City of Angels shares a great interest in the academic, as well as the spiritual, development of today's young people. To date, the church has helped fifty students to graduate from universities and colleges. These students have entered various fields of study. Currently there are thirty City of Angels students still attending institutions such as Harvard, University of Southern California, Spelman, Morehouse, Georgetown University,

University of California Berkeley, Colorado State University, San Diego State, University of California Santa Barbara, California State Northridge, Clark University, Drake, Florida State, California State University Los Angeles and others.

In 1987, The Rev opened Religious Science classes for one hundred members to teach the philosophy and concepts of the Science of Mind. The constant growth of the City of Angels Church of Religious Science created a need for a larger church home. Members continued to request more classes, more seminars, more office space and a place where they could have immediate access to books that supported their study of Religious Science.

In January of 1996, Rev. Dr. O. C. Smith, Robbie, and the congregation moved into their new church home at 5550 Grosvenor Boulevard, Los Angeles CA 90066. This was the perfect place, with a seating capacity of 1200, a stage with a cascading waterfall, offices, classrooms, and space for a bookstore and kitchen. Everyone rolled up their sleeves, broke out their paintbrushes and hammers, and began to beautify their new facility.

The dedication ceremony on March 6, 1996 was filled with music, entertainment, and great speakers, including Keynote Speaker Dr. Johnnie Colemon, founder of Christ Universal Temple in Chicago. The growth and development of the church increased, and this was the master plan for Rev. Dr. O. C. Smith. He said, "The church has been established for the purpose of aiding in the spiritual unfoldment and development of each individual that enters its door, for it is the place where God is worshiped."

The Rev said, "I've been many places. I've been to places you couldn't even find if you wanted to," as he smiled. Utilizing all forms of media, he reached out to those places to touch many people and teach them that they are God in expression. He taught this philosophy with great passion and affection. Anyone blessed to hear his message and meet him would be in 'awe' of the power he possessed. He reached millions of people around the world with his profound vision and voice. Dr. Smith lived his life with peace of mind, body, and spirit that can only be achieved with the intense focus and daily practice of the teaching he believed in, called the Science of Mind.

Rev. Dr. O. C. Smith extended his love and passion not only to his immediate family, the family of the City of Angels Church of Religious Science and the millions of people in the world. He touched everyone with his legacy and profound 'Voice' of love, peace, wellness and happiness. He has provided his family and the world with the tools to continue on their life's journey.

Rev. Smith has graduated to his next level of life. His loving wife, Robbie Gholson Smith; his daughters, Sherryn and Bonnie; his sons, Ocie Lee Kelly, Robert, Jesse, and Frank; his granddaughters, Monique, Jordan, Karisha, and Melonie; his grandsons, Sergio, Justin, Shawn, Frank, Tyler, Jesse, Myles, and Kelly—all will continue to celebrate his life and teachings.

JAMES E. SHAW, Ph.D

James Shaw has been a speechwriter for Chicago Cubs legend and Baseball Hall of Famer Ernie Banks and is a frequent media commentator who lectures throughout the United States on public school law and socially urgent issues regarding children and families.

A keynote speaker at the Columbine High School memorial ceremony, in Littleton, Colorado he earned his doctorate from the Claremont Graduate University and received Phi Delta Kappa's Best Dissertation of the Year award for 1997. In 2000, the California State Legislature honored him with its Certificate of Recognition for his writings on children and families.

A regular contributor to national publications, his previous books are *Jack and Jill, Why They Kill*; *Teaching Reading at Home*; and *We Love English!* (this last commissioned by the government of Japan). A school district administrator as well as an associate member of the American Bar Association and the Los Angeles Angeles County Bar Association, he resides in Los Angeles with his wife, Sylvia, who is a physician, and their three children.